The STAR Interview

How to tell a Great Story, Rock the Interview, and Land your Dream Job

www.starinterviewmethod.com

TABLE OF CONTENTS

BONUS MATERIAL

As a special gift to all my readers I've created a **free PDF** of 127 resources for your job search. It's a list that I wish I had several years ago when I was first interviewing — it would have made things a lot easier.

The PDF includes resume templates, time management tools, and apps to supercharge your job search.

Download the PDF here:
https://starinterviewmethod.com/bonusmaterial/

Why I Wrote this Book

Like most people, I've had good and bad experiences interviewing.

I once received a job offer and almost moved across the world, but the company suddenly withdrew their offer. Fortunately I hadn't moved yet. I still wonder, was it something I did that caused them to reconsider? They never told me, and to this day it's still a mystery.

Another time I wore a suit to an interview where everyone was wearing flip flops and shorts. It was uncomfortable, to say the least. And, perhaps not surprisingly, I didn't get the job.

I had another interview, with a company I knew nothing about. Halfway through the interviewer pulled out a strange-looking device (which looked like a vibrator) and asked me to "sell it" to them, as I was applying for a sales job. It turns out the product was a face-massager. Needless to say, I didn't get that job either.

And like most people, the whole job search process was usually a black box for me: complicated, mysterious, full of the unknown.

I didn't really understand how to find a job, the best way to interview, or how to make a positive impression. I read books, sure, but the advice they gave only went so far.

For the most part I had no idea what I was doing.

That was until I landed a job in the recruitment industry

where I stayed for over 4 years. I met with thousands of job seekers and dozens of CEO's. This opened up a whole new world for me. It was like opening Pandora's Box, but in a good way.

I gained a lot of perspective on how companies hire and what they truly value. I also got a lot of great experience helping people navigate through the job search process.

I realized that there's a pretty big gap between what job seekers are looking for and what companies are looking for. Each side has its own perspective, and this often causes a lot of issues — hiring mistakes, miscommunication, and ultimately, a lot of frustration.

Now my goal is to share what I've learned with as many people as I can.

Why? I believe transparency benefits everyone and increases the chances of achieving your goals. And that makes me happy.

How? I openly share interview advice on my blog and also write on Quora. And of course, in this book, I break down a lot of the concepts that I've learned over the years.

One of the most effective interview tools that I have found is the *STAR Method.*

STAR stands for:

- Situation
- Task
- Action
- Result

This is a technique to structure an answer and tell great stories. Although the method has been around for 20 years, it is more relevant today than ever. I didn't invent STAR Method — I just strapped a rocket to it and made it relevant to your job-seeking goals.

Now you might be thinking — *there are tons of techniques I can use, how is STAR different?*

Usually, in life there is one thing, one skill, or one action that acts as a cornerstone for everything else.

It follows the 80/20 rule, also known as the "Pareto principle." This means that 20% of your actions can produce 80% of your desired results.

Less effort, better results.

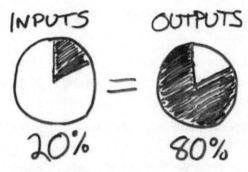

For example, perhaps you are always stressed and constantly make mistakes at work. You then add a few minutes of high-intensity exercise to your routine, which is a fraction of your daily schedule. Suddenly your anxiety is gone, you feel energized, and every aspect of your life is better. Your previous issues become miniscule. One small action can bring about big change and favorable results.

Since most companies use behavioral interview questions and are looking for detailed explanations of your history (stories), the STAR Method is going to work most of the time to address these two goals. It's that 20% you do that's going to give you the 80% of the result you're looking for.

Whether you're just starting your job search, already interviewing with a company, or looking for a different way to stand out — there are countless ways you can incorporate the technique into your life.

I've personally used the STAR Method for years to help hundreds of people find jobs at the world's biggest technology companies, like Facebook and Amazon.

I'm not saying this will solve 100% of your problems, but it's going to give you some serious bang for your buck.

Let's jump into it.

INTRODUCTION

Interviewing = Storytelling

Once upon a time, on a starry night, a caveman sat around a bonfire with his family and neighbors, and in his native dialect, grunted the events of the day. In other words, he told a story. And the story went a little like this:

My son and I were on our weekly hunt for wild boar, roughly four hundred steps from our village, toward the river. It had been several days since our last meal, and we were famished and eager to catch some fresh game. The heat of the sun pounded on us mercilessly.

Suddenly, we came face-to-face with a vicious, red-eyed lion. I froze, paralyzed for a moment.

I could tell it was thirsty for our blood. I felt my heart pounding through my chest and sweat dripping from my forehead. I glanced over at my son, who was terrified, and knew it was my responsibility to protect us. This was not the first time I had come across a lion, so I kept my composure, and mentally analyzed our options.

Option 1: Remain motionless until the lion went away. However, I wasn't sure if we could both remain calm in this situation.

Option 2: We could use our slingshots to scare off the lion. This would require good aim, which would prove very challenging, given my trembling hands. Of course, there was a good chance that I would miss, and just make the lion mad. Then he would then definitely attack us.

Option 3: I could punch the lion in the face. But even if I gathered enough nerve to do so, I would most likely get my hand bitten off.

Option 4: We could run to a nearby tree and climb out of the lion's reach. This seemed like the most reasonable option because the lion had not made a move yet, and the tree was less than a stone's throw away from us.

Alternatively, there was also a combination of these four options — but we didn't have much time to decide. I did a quick calculation of the distance between us and the tree and how fast the lion could bridge the gap. It was a rough estimate based on my eyewitness of lions chasing gazelles.

It was time for a decision. I decided we should go with the element of surprise, and shoot the lion with our slingshots first. This might give us enough time to run to the tree, even if I only stunned the lion momentarily.

I signaled to my son. We aimed our slingshots —BAM! Smack in the center of the lion's head.

Nice shot.

The lion was stunned. We raced to the trees and climbed to the top — safely! After the momentary shock wore off, the lion ran to the tree. But by that time we were high up in the branches and safe from the lion's sharp claws.

We waited until nightfall for the lion to go away and climbed back down the tree, returning to the village.

I learned that we should be more careful hunting wild boar during this time of day and this area because there were many lions around. It was an experience I certainly don't want to have again.

I also learned to always carry my slingshot.

Let's say our caveman friend was asked during an interview, *"tell me about a time when you faced a difficult situation."*

I think we can agree that he has a compelling story in response to that question.

It's descriptive, raw, and logical. It has a beginning, middle and end. We get the feeling that he can think on his feet and take action quickly. He didn't just say "we came across a scary lion and ran for our lives," even though that would also be an accurate, albeit a much less satisfying, answer. Rather, we understand exactly what he did, his decision-

8

making process, and how he analyzed and broke down a problem. There's even a "lesson learned," which shows that our ancestor was not only brave but also self-reflective. It may not be the most intellectually stimulating story, but it sure as hell answers the interviewer's question and puts them in the shoes of the caveman.

If our caveman was applying for a job as "Chief Security Officer" at a nearby village, we can be pretty confident that he would be invited to the next round of interviews.

Fortunately, our caveman friend never had to participate in an actual interview. He simply retold a true story based on events that happened to him, based on real facts and real people. Perhaps he embellished it a little bit to make it more entertaining for the crowd (for example, using descriptive words like "vicious", and describing the hunger in the lion's eyes), but it just gives the listener a better understanding of the environment and situation he faced.

Now let's fast forward a few thousand years to the present day.

The World is Unpredictable

You've developed a certain belief about interviewing over your lifetime, shaped by the media, people around you, and your own experiences.

When you think about interviewing, the following thoughts might come to mind:

- First impressions are important
- Data-driven examples

- Ugh, I am nervous and sweaty
- What the f*ck should I wear?
- Think on your feet
- Stuffy interview rooms
- Ask good questions
- Unfair labor practices
- Network
- Behavioral interviews
- Get referred by a friend who works at the company
- I hope I don't have to pee
- Write the perfect cover letter
- Trick questions that nobody could possibly answer

You were probably not consciously thinking about these things until I brought them up, but probably as I did your mind started to fill with related memories and feelings. You have certain beliefs about all of the above points. These beliefs shape your view and reaction to your environment. They exist regardless of whether you or not you acknowledge them.

The problem is that we can fall into certain patterns of thought without realizing it.

For example, you might subscribe to the belief that "good-looking people tend to get the job." Or you might have read the study that showed that having a symmetrical face could increase your chance of attaining wealth[i]. Or maybe you noticed that CEOs and successful people on the front page of the news always seem to be physically attractive.

There is certainly some truth to this. People who like one thing about you (your face) will tend to associate other good things with you, despite a lack of other supporting evidence. Also, if someone has a firm handshake, you might associate that with other positive traits. Such as, he is confident, or successful. Or perhaps if you hear that someone graduated from Harvard, it automatically evokes respect and you assume that they are intelligent, even though you have never met them before. This is referred to as the "halo effect."

However, there's a price we pay for falling for our own biases.

Situations and experiences will always change. There are interviewers who will not be distracted by your unusual facial features and will just listen to what you are saying. There are also interviewers who might do the opposite.

Ultimately, your beliefs become self-fulfilling prophecies. In this case, if you don't think you are "attractive" enough to be successful, then you subconsciously set yourself up for a downward spiral of negative thoughts.

On the other hand, if you think you are "attractive" and use it as a prop to maintain your confidence, you subconsciously set yourself up for disappointment when things don't go as planned.

I am not saying these biases don't exist. On the contrary — an infinite number of them exist!

The range of human experience and situations are so vast that it leaves the world open to much interpretation. There are simply too many factors at play for us to accurately predict outcomes consistently every time. A great example of this comes from trading in financial markets.

In a landmark study published years ago called "*Trading is*

Hazardous to your Wealth,"[ii] researchers found a startling fact after studying over 10,000 brokerage accounts. Professional traders whose job is to make money for their clients on average *lost* money by a substantial margin. The conclusion:

"Although professionals are able to extract a considerable amount of wealth from amateurs, few stock pickers, if any, have the skill needed to beat the market consistently, year after year. Professional investors, including fund managers, fail a basic test of skill: persistent achievement [....] The subjective experience of traders is that they are making sensible educated guesses in a situation of great uncertainty. In highly efficient markets, however, educated guesses are no more accurate than blind guesses."

Despite all of the skills, knowledge, and tools that these traders have, there are simply too many factors at play for them to beat the markets in the short term. The more actions (trades) they took, the worse it turned out for them. This is because their educated guesses were no more accurate than blind guesses, and at the end of the day it's a numbers game.

Interviewing is, of course, different than trading stocks.

First, obviously, people are not stocks. Past performance is an indicator of future events, generally speaking. If you run 10 miles every week for 15 weeks, most people would predict that on the 16th week you are probably going to run another 10 miles. If you always bite your nails before giving a speech, you'll probably bite your nails the next time you give a speech.

12

Second, in a job interview you have more control over the situation because you can directly influence the decision maker — they are sitting in front of you. You are not dealing with a black box (the market) of dozens of trades, where people can make random moves.

But there's still a great deal of uncertainty

Here are some of the ways that your job search, interview process and selection criteria could be totally random:

-*Interview Techniques*. A long-term study of job interview methods of Fortune 500 companies showed that most did not predict on the job performance after 1 year.[iii] This means that most of the new hires either did not perform as expected, left the company or were fired. The interviews were not indicative of their success on the job and were almost a random predictor. Companies could have randomly selected names from a hat and probably could have had more success in finding qualified employees.[iv]

-*Biological bias*. Your interview starts at 11am, right before lunch time. The interviewer's blood sugar level may be low, making them more irritable, distracted, hungry, and less likely to see you favorably. You could be 20% less likely to get the job than the person who interviews after lunch. (This was shown in study of Israeli judges who were less likely to grant parole to prisoners before lunchtime.)[v]

-*Lack of Clarity*. The interviewer did a poor job of defining the job description and has a fuzzy idea of the position expectations. This makes it difficult to assess what you have achieved, and the interviewer falls into "I have a good feeling about her" or "I have a bad feeling about him." This is mumbo-jumbo, and the interviewer will probably just choose someone who reminds them of themselves.

-*Timing.* You might be qualified to get a job and get through the interview with flying colors. But then, the company receives an internal application for the position you are interviewing for. Because it's cheaper for them to hire/transfer the person, they give the job to the internal candidate instead. Ouch.

These are just a handful of things that could happen in an interview that are out of your hands.

Once you realize the inherent bias in an interview, you can take some very simple steps. For example, you can schedule the interview after lunch when interviewers aren't distracted by their growling stomachs.

These are small things that you can do

However, most biases are not on *your* side so there's little you can do to change or influence them. It's hard enough to change our own biases, let alone those of others! There are simply too many factors to account for all of them. Changing human nature is nearly impossible.

While we live in a world that our ancestors even 100 years ago could not have imagined, the reality is that biologically, we haven't changed. We still fall prey to our own psychological fallacies. Indeed, we are apes living in a modern world.

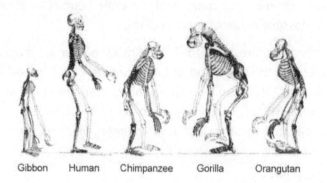

Gibbon   Human   Chimpanzee   Gorilla   Orangutan

With that said, let's find a different approach that doesn't require genetic modification.

This leads us back to our caveman and the power of stories.

You are sitting across the room from someone and having a conversation. You are assessing the atmosphere, establishing a connection, and trying to solve a real problem that the hiring managers have (they need to hire someone).

Enter Storytelling 101

How can you increase your chances of being selected for a job when interviewers all use different criteria for judgment and are slaves to their own unconscious prejudices?

There is no silver bullet approach. When you google "job interview advice" you will get 23,000,000 results. You'll need more than a couple of lifetimes to read all of that.

The best answer lies in creating a consistent framework that we can apply to all interviews, no matter what, that will maximize our chances of presenting ourselves as well as possible despite inherent biases.

When we are able to "cover most of our bases," we increase the likelihood of being understood. How do we do that? How can we make sure that we are heard in an interview and that we explain all of the relevant skills necessary for the job in a manner which is concise, compelling, and thorough?

We tell stories.

Yes, stories.

<u>When we tell detailed stories with precision and relevance, we increase our chances of being selected for the job, based on our own experience. Even if you are nervous or awkward, if you can effectively communicate how you earned your previous company X amount of dollars, people are going to listen.</u>

The interviewer might not like your haircut or maybe your handshake was kind of limp (it happens). It doesn't matter. If you can provide enough relevant information to show that you can do the job, you can change their perception of you.

By painting a great picture of events while including a subjective storyline and objective facts, we minimize the external biases that can get in the way of out evaluation. Even if the interviewer is not impressed by our wardrobe, he can see our thought process, and understand how and why we take actions.

We can connect with people on a logical *and* emotional level. Winning the hearts and minds of people is the best thing we can hope to do.

Storytelling is the human answer to operating in an environment full of bias.

Before we move on let me summarize the following concepts that we've established:

- We cannot account for all of the biases that an interviewer has. Interviewing techniques are random.
- Past performance is a good indicator of our future performance. How you do *anything* is how you do *everything.*
- Sharing stories about our past job performance (in a structured and detailed manner) can help mitigate the inherent biases we will encounter in an interview.

Why are stories so powerful?

We've been telling stories since the advent of the spoken word. Storytelling and knowledge sharing were key to our survival; passing along ideas, wisdom, and secrets.

Humans are emotional creatures. We are deeply moved by a tale of a girl who barely escaped with her life at the hands of a Nazi soldier. But when we hear facts like *"millions of people died,"* the *people* just become another statistic that we cannot fathom. We remain emotionless in the face of numbers and the meaning is stripped away.

Airbnb started modestly - just a couple of guys running it

with practically no money and no product, trying to build something on the idea of 'opening up and sharing your home with others,' going against centuries of tradition.

Their first ever 'pitch deck' developed by the 3 founders shared a powerful story about the problem they were solving and they had the market data to support it.[vi] Eventually they raised millions of dollars in venture capital funding and expanded to over 50 countries in just 5 years, without owning any physical assets. It takes a very carefully and well-orated story to convince someone that your idea, which is just an idea at this point, is going to be worth millions or billions of dollars in the future.

Stories have taught us much of what we know about the world. For example, how do you know anything about what police work is like? What's the process for a criminal investigation or court hearing? We've seen these situations on fictional shows like *CSI or Dexter.* What would we know about the life of poor Indian children living in the slums or life in Afghanistan, if it were not for books like *Slumdog Millionaire* and *The Kite Runner*? Books, movies, shows and videos shape our view of the world, regardless of how accurate or inaccurate they may be.

We huddle in blankets, peeking through our fingers to catch a glimpse of the grisly murder scene about to occur on the TV screen. We know that movies are not real and that the actors are acting their part, but we *feel* as if they are real, and we respond physiologically through sweating, gasping, and yelling *"run for God's sake, run you idiot, you're going to die!"*

What about the darker side of storytelling? How is it

possible for an entire nation to be hypnotized by an art-school dropout with a funny mustache, who proclaimed war against humanity in the name of the Aryan race? How was he able to convince his followers to kill millions of people in a global bloodbath that shaped the course of human history forever? Hitler spent hours in front of the mirror practicing his speeches. While undeniably evil, he was one of the greatest storytellers of all time.

It's clear that stories have the power to sculpt our imaginations and beliefs.

More importantly, all of this has a biological basis. Evolution has wired our brains to respond to stories and it has been shown that stories can influence our personality and form our opinions on everything from sex, race, violence, and ethics.[vii]

With a story, you can influence others to 'experience' something that you have experienced. In neuroscience this is referred to as "neural coupling" and it means that the listener's brain activity closely mirrors the speaker's brain activity. You're literally communicating on the same wavelength through the power of a story.

In one landmark neurological study, scientists found that:

Communication is a shared activity resulting in a transfer of information across brains. The findings shown here indicate that during successful communication, speakers' and listeners' brains exhibit joint, temporally coupled, response patterns [...] Interestingly, some of these extralinguistic areas are known to be involved in processing social information crucial for successful communication, including, among others, the capacity to discern the beliefs, desires, and goals of others. [viii]

This has huge implications for how we present ourselves in an interview. If we can become good storytellers, then we can become good at influencing, convincing, and persuading.

When we can tell a good story, we can connect with people and increase the chance that they will understand what we're *really* trying to say.

What's in a story?

Years ago, while I was in college, I was applying for my first sales job. It paid very well (for a college student) and was notoriously difficult to get into, so I spent time crafting a very long cover letter with a descriptive story about my childhood. When I was a kid I would gather and spray-paint pine cones, then sell them around our neighborhood during Christmas time for a quarter a piece. I linked this story to my *creativity, tenacity, and sales ability*.

Really, I was just a bored kid with lots of pinecones in my backyard. But I was selected for an interview and they specifically commented on my story. Ultimately, I got hired for the job.

You might be thinking, *"That's great, but I'm not a good storyteller. I don't have any interesting stories."*

The fact that you are alive on this planet means you have a story to tell. It doesn't have to be over the top and full of wild gestures, nor does it have to be perfectly delivered. Using a mix of well-timed gestures and powerful words can help, but they're just part of the equation.

The key for storytelling in the context of a job interview is providing the right amount of relevant detail, in a structured format that makes sense. The words you choose matter and the relevant detail is key. You can add the cherry on top later.

You see, here's the caveat with storytelling in the context of an interview: It's not quite the same as other types of storytelling.

There's a subtle difference.

You can be a great speaker and have excellent delivery, but your story could lack substance. You could even appear very confident when you answer your questions, but your answers could be surface-level and fail to get to a deeper or relevant point. Or it could be an emotionally appealing story and make people cry.

But we're talking about interviews here, not coming up with a Pulitzer prize-winning story.

In fact, this is where problems arise and where hiring mistakes are made. In the case of a "convincing" storyteller, he or she can bullshit their way through an interview. They get hired for the job, but then are gone within 6 months.

The purpose of telling a story is different depending on the situation. If you are telling a story to your friends, doing a speech for a TED talk or just recounting a funny story at a party, your goals are probably going to be different in all of these situations. Maybe you're just trying to get something off your chest or get a laugh out of someone.

If you are telling a story in a job interview, your goal is to make sure that the interviewer understands you 100%, so that you can get the job.

In order to tell this type of story you need three things:

- You have to pack your story with highly-relevant information. Facts.
- At the same time, you want to elicit a "neural coupling" response so that the interviewer connects with you on a deeper level and gets the emotional connection.
- You want to have three, four, or more stories in mind. That way you can pick and choose relevant stories depending on the context.

A STAR "story" for our purposes is going to be about your experiences. It's about how you did something, why you did something, and deconstructing all of the details around that.

The point is you don't need to have unwavering confidence, a great voice, or perfectly-timed hand gestures. Those are just nice-to-haves.

Fighting Human Nature with Human Nature

What is it about a story that breaks through a person's bias?

A story is designed partially to answer the questions and partially for emotional appeal. It's very possible, and likely, that the interviewer is going to ask you follow-up questions. It's not just about motives. It's about your logic. It's about numbers. It's about your deductive reasoning in particular situations. Remember, they are looking at your past performance.

It's often said that the fear of public speaking has its roots in biology. Having so many pairs of eyes staring at us triggers a reminiscent evolutionary response akin to the hungry gaze of a predatory lion. No wonder we get sweaty and nervous — we want to *escape from potential death.*

Interviewing elicits a similar response. The fear of public speaking is probably greater, but interviewing is also seen as "unnatural" and a skill that needs to be honed.

Countless books have been written about interviewing. How to answer certain questions, how to avoid a faux-pas, how to master behavioral interviews, group interviews -- you name it.

There is some great advice in these books, but often they over-complicate things or cover them with an air of mystique. Also, the amount of information out there can be overwhelming. The first thing we should do is to detach ourselves from the word "interviewing." I'll use it interchangeably with storytelling, but note that I'm talking about the same thing. Storytelling is not as mysterious as it seems.

Now we know that...

Interviewing is full of human bias. And we can't change human nature (eh, I know the scientists are working on it and inevitably we *will.* I get it. But for now, we're 21st century beings stuck in bodies that have been shaped over millions of years of evolution, so we have to deal with the biases that come with that).

Humans will respond to a great story because we are hardwired to do so. We know that we cannot overcome human bias so the best way to fight it is by being as human as possible.

Sharing descriptive and thorough stories is a great way to overcome the inherent bias in interviews, and thus act as an effective way to increase our chances of success.

Knowing this, we can start to form our own stories using STAR.

What is STAR?

The STAR Interview, or as I like to call it, STAR *storytelling* method, is a way to answer questions. It's a way to structure your examples in an interview. It's also an outline for telling an effective story and I believe it is the *one thing* that is going to knock it out of the park for you. It's that 20% thing you do that's going to give you 80% of the results you're looking for.

There are four steps:

- Situation
- Task
- Action
- Result

Easy, right?

There are many companies, (Amazon is a great example) who explicitly recommend STAR as the best preparation tool for their interviews. And although not all companies specifically talk about using STAR, most companies, including many Fortune 500 companies, use some method of behavioral interviewing.

A "behavioral interview" is a type of interview which tries to assess your past behavior in order to predict your fit for the job. It means they want to hear stories about your past, which might indicate your ability to do the job you are interviewing for. All of these companies are essentially saying one thing:

"Please, oh please, tell us a good story!"

The best way to answer behavioral interview questions is with the STAR technique.

However, it's important to note that past performance does not mean that you have experience taking on the exact responsibilities of a new position.. In fact, even if you've just graduated, and have absolutely no work experience, or are switching industries midway through your career, companies can assess your past performance. But how?

Cheri Huber, Zen Buddhist meditation teacher and author sums it up nicely, *"How you do anything is how you do everything."* When you describe your leadership role on the tennis team at the university, it reflects your leadership ability. When you organized a large event for a political campaign as an intern, it shows your organizational ability. When you worked 3 part-time jobs to fund your education, it shows your grit and work ethic. When you broke the sales record at your previous company, it shows that you know a thing or two about sales.

All of these examples and more can be told in the format of a story. Companies have certain "job requirements" in mind when assessing candidates. However, they use these requirements (usually written on a job description) as more of a guideline. That's why you should not get hung up on every single detail of a job description. In reality the majority of companies are looking for *transferable* skills from your life and work experiences.

Thus, the importance of being able to tell a story in relation to what you might be doing on the job is one of the best ways to show interviewers you are capable. Of course, you might have specific experience or achievement that indicates, "Yes, I've done this before." However, it's unlikely that all of the details are spelled out on your resume, so greater *context* is necessary in order to explain the relevance. This is where your storytelling powers come in.

With a good story you will be able to answer questions such as, "Tell me about a time when you had to show leadership" or "what was your biggest achievement?"

Like any good story, you need to start by painting a picture of what happened, where you were, and the people involved. This is the *situation*. There likely was something that was required or expected of you. You have to identify what this is and describe it clearly. This is the *task*. Once you've decided the goal or outcome you would like to achieve, you need to take steps to get there. What steps did you take and why did you take them? That's the *action*. After moving forward with your plan, what happened? Were you successful, and what did you learn? This is the *result*.

Let's break it down using our caveman example.

Situation: *My son and I were hunting wild boars and suddenly came across a lion. Our lives were in danger.*

Task: *The goal was to find a way to escape, so I analyzed one of 4 options. As the elder, it was my duty.*

Action: *We decided to shoot the lion with our sling shot and make a run for the tree.*

Result: *We survived! I learned that we shouldn't hunt in that area, and to always carry a slingshot.*

It doesn't matter if you are a caveman sharing a story about escaping a lion, or if you're a marketing manager talking about your most successful marketing campaign. The STAR Method is not industry-specific and can be used to frame all of your examples to make them more structured and compelling.

Where can you use STAR?

Ten or twenty years ago the most efficient thing you could do was use STAR to structure your response in an interview. It was a fun interview technique, but not critical to your success in an interview.

Nowadays, the landscape is different. Stories are more important than ever and STAR is even more relevant today than it was 20 years ago.

That's because the workplace has changed dramatically in the past few years. Think about this:

-The International Labor Organization estimates that 75% of workers **in the entire world** are employed on temporary or part time contracts.[ix] Currently there are 55 million freelancers in the U.S. It's expected that by 2020 over 40% of Americans will have freelancing jobs.[x]

-Companies are risk-averse after the 2008 economic crisis. They don't want to hire full time workers and would rather hire part time or project workers. It's more cost effective. This means jobs are less secure.[xi]

-Jobs are being disrupted, evolving or disappearing altogether. As Marc Andreesen famously said, "software is eating the world." 10 years ago we didn't have Uber drivers, YouTubers, driverless car engineers or social media managers. Today these are sought-after positions with unique skills.

-It's hard to stand out in such a rapidly changing world. You can send hundreds of resumes and get no response. Any employer can Google your name and search your LinkedIn, Facebook and Twitter. They make an immediate judgment based on your online presence. Google is your new resume.[xii]

-The nature of education is changing and the value of a standard degree is steadily declining. Nowadays potential employees have access to great resources online with services like Skillshare, Udemy and Khan Academy.[13]

In a day and age when virtually everyone around us has access to the same information online, how are we supposed to stand out? When our jobs are not secure and people are shifting to multiple streams of income, or the 'gig economy,' how do we stand out?

You guessed it — stories.

Yes, you can use STAR stories for any situation to do all the following:

- Reach out and apply to companies during your job search
- Interview for a full-time or part-time job
- Get yourself noticed as a freelancer
- Consulting gigs
- Write a badass LinkedIn profile
- Make a great blog or portfolio
- Network

If any (or all) of these sound like your goals, start using STAR.

Two types of job seekers

A top executive recruiter at Amazon told me about the two types of candidates that she has encountered over the years. She interviewed thousands of people and hired many. There are many personalities, strengths, weaknesses, and other traits. But usually she noticed that people fall into two categories that ultimately determine their success in the interview process.

Type #1: This person sees themselves as the victim. The employer they are interviewing with cannot be trusted because they are trying to weed people out of the interview process or might low-ball them on a job offer. They proceed cautiously. They are not open to feedback and do not accept the fact that interview preparation will take hours and is not something that will just come naturally. This person might be a good storyteller, but that doesn't mean they are telling the right stories. They might have a lot of years of great work experience which allows them to believe that they are naturally good at interviewing. They are surprised when they don't called back for the second interview.

Type #2: This person knows that they don't know. They may or may not have a strong understanding of their own background. They may or may not be confident in how they express themselves. But they are open to learning about an individual company's interview process and can take constructive feedback from recruiters and hiring managers. They are always prepared. They realize that no matter how much job experience they have, they might not be a naturally great interviewee. They spend hours and hours preparing for interviews and are constantly learning. They are the ones who get the job despite not being the loudest in the room.

The point is that it doesn't matter how much experience you have. It doesn't matter if you have even interviewed hundreds of people yourself, as a manager. You're sitting on the other side of the table now. In fact, those who have a lot of experience interviewing others inevitably get used to a certain "style" of interviewing that may not be current or relevant. All of us have to hone our approach and remain adaptable.

What the STAR Method is NOT

We are using STAR in the context of behavioral interviewing, *"Tell me about a time when..."* It doesn't necessarily mean that you will be the subject of the example, but it's going to inevitably be about *your* experience. That's the whole point.

It's not going to help you answer a question like *"How would you construct a fishing net that can cover the Pacific Ocean?"* And honestly, if someone asks you that question, ask them how on earth that's relevant to the job, and if that is an actual project you'd be working on.

You can use elements of STAR to structure your response, or to think about a similar problem you have solved in the past. But unless it's something you've done before, then a story format is not going to make sense — you need to problem-solve.

What the STAR Method *will* do is allow you to answer most questions in an interview in a compelling way.

Summary

#1: Don't get too tied up on the word "interviewing." It's basically storytelling and we can apply STAR to a variety of situations.

#2: Accept that we operate in a world full of biases, different situations, and different experiences that are unpredictable.

#3: Stories have been told since the beginning of time and remain an effective way to communicate about our past.

#4: Use the STAR Method to tell a good story AND get your point across. Maximize your chances of success.

How to Use This Book

Each chapter contains examples and tips to construct every step of your STAR story. We'll start with a brainstorming session, break down each step of STAR, and then piece it all together. There are exercises and practice prompts throughout so you can formulate your STAR stories throughout the book.

By the end of the book you'll have over 55 stories to share during your job interview.

I've tried to keep my examples broad and industry-neutral. At the end of the book, I also provide a list of resources, STAR examples, books and other tools that should prove useful in your journey to master storytelling. **Let's get to it!**

CHAPTER 1:

BRAIN DUMP

Imagine yourself dumping out all of your ideas and experiences onto a sheet of paper.

Visualized it?

Good, now we want to get all of our ideas down on a piece of paper to start the thinking process. Here's how we're going to do it:

1. Think of the "greatest achievement" that you've had in your career or life up to this point. This is a great starting point because you'll always be asked this question in some form. If you don't have a great achievement from the workplace, think back to internships or something you did in school. Don't get bogged down with the idea that it has to be "momentous" like rescuing a baby from a burning building or making your company a billion dollars, or some other Herculean act.

It can be simple. For example, a time when you came up with a suggestion or idea which was implemented. Anything that you are proud or excited about that you have done. You can download a template for shaping this story from the resources page on https://starinterviewmethod.com/resources/

2. Now that you've thought of an example write down everything you can remember about the achievement. I mean everything. Don't worry about putting it into a STAR format or making it pretty or structured; only you are going to be reading this. Just jot down or type out a bunch of notes.

3. Don't be afraid to include minute details, as well as the bigger picture.

4. Great, now this is your starting point. Save this. We will use it to refine the situation, task, action and result in the next chapters.

Next, let's get organized.

I suggest creating an Excel sheet that looks like the example below (or writing it out on paper). You can use this document to keep track of all of our examples. Here's a link to a template you can download. https://starinterviewmethod.com/resources/

We'll use this to write down the bulk of our STAR stories.

Why Details Matter

You're probably wondering *"why in the heck do I need to recall all of this information?"*

Of course, some things that may not ultimately matter -- for example, we don't need to know the weather during the day your example takes place.

You want to put in all of the details that contribute to the story in a meaningful way, but not more than that. "Meaningful" details relate directly to the job.

This also doesn't mean that your story will always end up super detailed. On the contrary, it's the simplest and most concise stories that will stick.

In fact, **your entire STAR story should only be 3-5 minutes long at most.** No one has time for a story that drags on for much longer. However, you will have enough details to construct many, many more stories.

Having many details on hand will allow you to have a lot of flexibility to create different stories depending on what interview questions you will be asked.

The logical flow is equally important.

In his book "Principles," billionaire hedge-fund manager Ray Dalio describes his approach to synthesizing ideas that have different levels. This can be used for decision making, telling a story, and making a point.

Letters A through G represent your main points, and "synthesis" is your conclusion of those points. The numbers 1-5 represent details for each main point.

This would be a logical way to get to your point from A to G:

A →	B →	C →	D →	E →	F →	G →	Synthesis
1	1	1	1	1	1	1	
2	2	2	2	2	2	2	
3	3	3	3	3	3	3	
4	4	4	4	4	4	4	
5	5	5	5	5	5	5	

You've also probably had the experience of telling a story or trying to explain something but then getting side-tracked, or "bogged down in the details."

If you find yourself getting too deep into the details, you can lose track of your initial point and then end on an irrelevant point without explaining the full picture.

That would look something like this:

A →	B →	C	D	E	F	G	
1	1 ↓	1	1	1	1	1	
2	2 ↓	2	2	2	2	2	
3	3 ↓	3 →	3 →	3	3 ↑	3 →	No Synthesis
4	4	4	4 .↓	4 →	4 →	4	
5	5	5	5	5	5	5	

Now, we want our story to successfully get from point A to B and onwards. In the context of STAR, the "A" would be Situation, "B" would be Task, "C" would be Action, "D" would be Result, and perhaps "E" would be lessons learned.

Sometimes we'll need to dive deep, other times we won't.

When we know A through G and 1 through 5, we can do a great job of painting the bigger picture as well as providing the deepest level of detail when necessary.

This is why details matter.

Now that we've jotted down everything we can remember about our greatest accomplishment (or whatever example you chose), we can start structuring it and refining it with the *Situation*.

CHAPTER 2:

SITUATION

Describe a specific event or situation that you were in. Be sure to provide enough context and detail for the listener to understand. Never assume. The situation can be from a previous job, volunteer experience or any related event.

> *"To hell with facts! We need stories!"*
> -Ken Kesey

STARting the Story

In order for us to create a good story and make it relevant (and not too long), we're going to gather some key pieces of information from the interviewer.

What is the interviewer or listener really looking for?

There are a dozen places that you can start your story, and the "best" place will depend on the amount of context you have received from the interviewer. But since you're just starting, wouldn't the amount of context be zero?

No, because you should have a lot of information already.

If you don't, here are some points that you can research

and questions to ask yourself before stepping into the interview.

- Information about the company (size of the company, growth, their products/services)
- The job description (what skills are listed)
- Roles and responsibilities (what specific things will you be doing)
- Their biggest "pain point" (why are they looking for this hire?)
- Information about the interviewer (if you can find it on LinkedIn)

The best place to start is usually a simple, declarative statement explaining where you were and where you worked.

Depending on the complexity of the question, your entire STAR story shouldn't be more than 2-5 minutes.

That leaves roughly thirty seconds to one minute to describe the situation, which should be plenty of time to start your answer to something like *"what was your biggest achievement?"* You can simply start out with *"At the time I worked at x company during X time as a marketing manager. My task was to.."*

And we're already off into the *task* in just a few seconds.

Understandably the situation could be a lot more complex and thus require a few minutes. If you are a lawyer and trying to set the scene for a case that you spent months working on, you need to get the details right.

But within the context of your story, be as concise as you can.

Peeling the Layers off the Onion

The situation is where you start to paint a picture. You will set the tone for the rest of the story. It's important that you make it juicy from the start -- you're probably the umpteenth candidate the interviewer has seen today, and they can't wait to get home and watch Game of Thrones, so you have less than 30 seconds to catch their attention.

Go.

Here are all of the elements that will uncover the true meaning of your situation. Looking at your "great achievement" example that you just spewed out all over your computer or notebook, you can now refine the first part of it.

Ask yourself the following questions and write down the answers in the STAR template provided above.

1.Where on earth were you?

What was the name of the company or your role/specific title at the time? How much revenue did the company bring in last year? Were you working in a team? How many employees did they have? What was the company's business model, in a nutshell? What was the culture like?

2.Timeframe, year, month, date.

Did you join the company recently? How many years ago was this? Is the season important somehow? Probably not, leave it out. You don't need to give an exact date and time but providing some reference of time will help the listener with the time frame.

3. Why am I in this situation?

Why were you involved in this situation and not someone else? What incentives were in place for you? Was there something worth mentioning that caused you to end up here?

4. Who were the people involved?

What were the names and titles of the people involved? What was your relationship with these individuals?

5. What is the problem? What happened? Why did it happen?

Explain the specific problem in one, concise sentence. *"Our event venue canceled at the last minute, so we had to find another venue within 48 hours."* You might want to explain why this happened if it's important. In the event venue example, do we need to know? Maybe, maybe not. Did you personally misunderstand the venue date when making the reservation (your fault, in which case you might want to mention that) or were there some factors simply beyond your control (venue overbooked by accident, in which case it's probably not important for the listener)?"

6. What was your responsibility at the time?

What was your function and how did you spend your days? Was this situation different to what you usually faced, and were you equipped to handle the situation? Had you faced it many times before or was this the first time?

7. What was the microclimate (of the business)?

This means providing context beyond the details above. The "micro-" refers to the local situation in your company, your personal life, your city. For example, perhaps the company recently hired a new CEO. Perhaps people are nervous or unhappy with this situation, and it has affected their work. Maybe you just go promoted internally, and you're swamped with new training requirements. How do these factors influence the situation? If they don't, leave them out.

8. What was the macroclimate?

What were the big external events that might have influenced your current situation? If you worked for an airline company during the Icelandic volcanic eruptions, it was probably a pretty busy time for you.

9. What were you thinking and feeling?

Upon describing the details around the problem, you can dive deeper into your initial reaction to what happened and the situation you were faced with. *"My initial reaction was fear. I was scared of losing my job. It was mentally tough, but I quickly put emotions aside and moved to determine what my options were..."* This helps show how you react to the situation and your internal thinking process (and how you might react in a similar situation). It's a peek into your mind. This will segue quickly into the *Tasks*.

10. What information is relevant and what information is irrelevant? Leave out the irrelevant.

Once you get your whole story mapped out, you can

work backward to double check that there aren't any unnecessary details.

So, to summarize, your situation should include the following:

- Where was it
- When was it
- Why did it happen
- What happened
- Who was involved
- Macro/Micro climate
- What were you feeling

Let's put this into practice. Here's an example *situation* about 'setting a goal and achieving it' during university.

I have always been very active in extracurricular school activities back in college. I was a Political Science major at the University of Oregon and enjoyed debates/discussions, reading news, and sports. I was also a consistently on the dean's list. But the one subject that I hated, and always underperformed in, was math. I had a math teacher back in high school whom I didn't get along with, so I probably held onto some resentment from that time. Anyway, it was my final year of university, and I still had to complete one business course to graduate, so as you can imagine I was quite stressed. If I didn't pass, I would have been required to take a summer course and delay my graduation date.

And that's it for the situation. Short and sweet.

Remember, STAR is just a way to structure your stories. The stories can be anything from an internship, part-time work, a life event, and school. There are no limits.

Context is Key

Let's say you've been living in Indonesia and working at an ecommerce company called GoJek for the past five years of your life. Now you are interviewing for a job at Facebook Headquarters in Menlo Park and explaining how you built a marketing strategy for one of your new products.

<u>Without providing context from the start, you risk losing the interviewer or missing a big opportunity to win from the beginning.</u> The interviewer might not fully understand the scope of your company, for example. He might not know that GoJek is like the Uber of Indonesia, competes with Apple Pay, and has grown by 500% in the past two years.

It doesn't matter if you are interviewing with someone that you "think" clearly knows about your company, or has heard of them. I don't care if it's Microsoft or Google. It's important to share relevant information so that they are totally clear. You need to remind the interviewer.

"While Microsoft is a large company, I was actually working in the Xbox division before we launched, so it was basically a startup operation."

And if it's not a huge company, then it's even more critical that you share details about the company. How big is the company regarding headcount? What were their revenue figures? What was the culture like? What was your position?

After taking all these points into account, here's what my opening description of the situation would look like:

At the time I was working as a cyber security manager at Skynet, which is the only company in the world that produces flying cybernetic robots capable of time-travel for military use. We had about 2000 people and brought in 1 billion USD in revenue last year. It was a very organized and top-down structured business.

On Christmas Day we detected a critical breach of the system — it was a Russian cyber hacking attack. My role was to manage a team of network engineers, and our mission was to make sure our internal network remained impenetrable to attack. Most people in my 40-person team were off on holiday, so I had to spring into action immediately despite limited resources.

If you've watched the *Terminator,* then I wouldn't have to tell you much about my fictitious company, Skynet. But I will always take the safe route and explain the business anyway, just in case you haven't heard of Skynet.

Don't Assume Anything

In my previous sales job when we would close a deal and record the information on our Customer Relationship Management (CRM) system, internally we would refer to this as "popping." If someone were to walk into our office at the end of the month you'd overhear people saying things like, *"when are you going to pop her?"* and *"Excited to pop today!"*

Scandalous.

Our jobs come with individual jargon, so we become accustomed to talking a certain way. Catch yourself when you do this and provide context or else you will be left with blank stares, or even worse, the interviewer will just pretend to understand what you said as you continue to talk, which will confuse them even more.

You know what they say about assumptions. They make an *ass*, out of *you* and *me*.

How much is too much?

Spending 5 minutes painting a scenario is almost always unnecessary. You will risk sounding verbose and possibly get lost in your description, forgetting your point. I've seen this happen many times. Sometimes the interviewer will stop the person, but other times they will let them ramble on. The interviewee doesn't get the job, and the feedback is "they couldn't get to the point."

This can be avoided.

How you do the following is going to depend on the specific job you are interviewing for. You are talking about what makes sense contextually in *that specific meeting.*

For example, if you are interviewing for a startup company you might want to emphasize the entrepreneurial nature of your greatest achievement or how you took on several responsibilities with little supervision. Because that's what it's like at a startup. And maybe you don't emphasize the fact that you have three bosses and 50,000 employees.

Using the above guidelines here are a few simple tricks to start refining your STAR answer and tailoring it to each specific interview situation/company that you will face.

Cut the fat. At first, we want to write down as many details as possible when we are going through preparing our STAR stories because our minds work by association. When one neuron fires closely to other neurons that are connected to an idea or sensation from that experience, you can refresh your memory on the details then you'll be able to better retell your story. This is referred to as a "neural network" and has been well-documented in neurobiology.[xiii] You'll be able to answer the "why" questions or the inevitable question of certain details that are asked.

Our first step to refining our *situation* is to keep in mind the size of the company, type of business, and macro/micro factors that could be relevant. Ask yourself, *"How will this be relevant in the job? Is it similar in any way to what the job description says?"*

Ask questions. There is no rule that your STAR story has to be a monologue. **In fact, it's almost always better to intermittently elicit small responses from your interviewer to keep them feeling engaged.** The easiest way to understand or clarify if someone got your point, or if they need more context, is simply stop during your story and to ask them. In describing an example to hit a tight deadline during your time at a newspaper publisher, you might quickly ask *"Are you familiar with the workflow in news publishing?"* If the interviewer is very familiar, then you can summarize and move on, but if they're not, you'll have to lay things out for them in more detail.

Facial gestures and body language. This is a more practical in-interview tip. I would hope that people aren't as rude to glance at their watches to indicate their boredom. (Do people do that?) Maybe, but usually, they're more subtle. They might just nod their head, give you a blank stare, or indicate slight impatience with "Yep, yep, I see." If you notice this, the interviewer may just be a jerk, or you might need to speed up.

Don't forget about culture. Interviewers are not always good at interviewing, and very few are good at asking questions. The complexity of this increases when considering communication between cultures and non-native English speakers.

For example, Japan is a high-context culture that expects people to *"read between the lines"* in almost every situation. In this case, you will not hear many Japanese people blatantly saying "yes" or "no". Instead, they will find a roundabout way to decline an invitation or a softer way to show their excitement. Whereas in the US, not speaking up might be seen as a sign of weakness, in Japan it is seen as a sign of humility. Being too loud, excited or aggressive in Japan would conversely be seen as negative.

Keep these cultural contexts in mind when you are speaking to your interviewer. There's no way to know for certain what they are thinking, but before diving into your STAR story, you can give a tiny snippet of what you are going to discuss. *"Oh sure, I have a good story about a deadline I had to meet in my previous job about ten years ago during my time as a marketing associate. Would that be a relevant example?"* Their response might be "yes", or they might ask for a more recent example during your time as a manager. *The point is, you don't know until you ask.*

Three Ways to be Concise

Skip unnecessary details. When first crafting the situation part of your STAR story, you should write down as much detail as possible. This will help make sure that you capture all of the key pieces and that you may or may not need. Once you have this covered, you can eliminate all of the unnecessary details depending on the context of the question and the context of the person with whom you are speaking.

Don't think out loud. Before starting your example, using words like "umm" and "hmm" and "yeah, let's see..." is going to make it seem like you're uncertain, might not have prepared, or that you don't have a good example. There is nothing wrong with taking a couple of minutes to gather your thoughts. Instead of thinking out loud you can say, *"Sure, give me a second to think of a good example."*

The rule of 3's. When answering any question that has several answers like *"what were the key factors to your success in the project?"* or *"What do you think makes a good manager based on your experience?"* I recommend using the rule of 3s, that is, listing three things that qualify you. No more and no less. Thomas Jefferson and Steve Jobs have both used this technique. For some reason, our minds gravitate towards this number. Having two reasons doesn't seem like enough, and having four or five reasons seems like a little bit too much. If you can squeeze it down to three reasons or three points, it'll sound like you know your stuff. Like this section, it has 3 points. Coincidence? I think not.

Stylistic Tips

Don't use fancy words. Often people try to display their vocabulary prowess, thinking it will leave a good impression. This almost always has the opposite effect as it can seem to the other person like you are trying to show that you are superior, by distinguishing your eloquent verbosity from their paltry parlance.

The point of the story is not to brag, but to communicate your point to someone sitting across the table from you. If a six-year-old can't understand what you are saying, it's unlikely that you'll catch the attention of your interviewer, let alone impress them.

Eye contact. What is the right amount of eye contact without coming off as creepy? Staring directly into someone's eyes is going to give off a weird vibe, or might come off as too aggressive. Looking away will make you seem shy, feeble, or like you are hiding something. My tip is to make eye contact every 3 seconds or so. When you hit an emotional climax in your story, I would suggest looking up at the interviewer. *"The company lost 500,000 dollars, and it was my fault."* If you were to say this sentence while looking down at the floor, it might indicate that you are ashamed of what you've done and have not gotten over the pain of the issue. There is nothing wrong with pain. But when you face up to it and make eye contact, the interviewer will be able to feel your pain. That's a good thing.

Mirroring. Verbal language only represents a small part of communication -- something like 80% of communication is body language. Studies have shown that mirroring the body language of your interviewer can make them see you more positively.[xiv]

Hand gestures. Also referred to as *gesticulation*, one of my favorite words. (Remember that's gesticulation with a G, not a T.) I've interviewed people that throw their hands around and make wild movements to describe uneventful situations. *The marketing budget at the time was huge, I mean, it was in the millions of dollars (stretching his arms widely across the room like an eagle). I mean, really big, like this big!*

If you sit with your arms crossed (which I see people do inadvertently), you'll come off as closed and unwelcoming. I remember I used to swivel back and forth in chairs. It's a bad habit; maybe you have it too. I had to try really hard to remember not to swivel around and sit still, but it made it a lot easier when I just focused on what the interviewer was doing and copied that.

The best thing you can do is to mirror the body language of the interviewer because you will come across as more relatable. Salespeople use this technique to sell, and psychologists use this as a technique to make people feel more at ease. You can use it too.

You don't need to overdo it. Conversely, staring tuna-faced at the person in front of you and keeping your hands in your pockets is also unlikely to flatter anyone. You are not a tuna.[xv]

A good habit is keeping your hands flat on the table in front of you or in plain sight. This has a positive psychological impact that builds trust. When someone is hiding their hands we sense that they are hiding *something.* It's similar to crossing your arms; it gives off a vibe that you are closed and not forthcoming. Opening up your chest and keeping your hands in sight are two basic tactics that you can use to build trust with someone.

The easiest and most natural time to make a gesture is when you are describing something that requires counting, like the rule of 3's mentioned above. Another good time to gesticulate is when you are describing a scene of some sorts. In the description above about the large marketing budget, it's completely appropriate to make some sort of gesture to emphasize how big the budget was (just not a huge eagle spreading one). Unless the interview takes place in Italy, a simple movement of your hands will suffice.

Inevitably they will look at your hands a couple of times (make sure they're clean) as you gesticulate. If you find that the interviewer keeps staring at your hands or gestures, this might be a sign they are getting distracted, and you might be overdoing it.

Bad Examples

"John, tell me about the time you handled a challenge."

"When the software development of our new product stalled, I coordinated the team which managed to get the schedule back on track. We were able to successfully troubleshoot the issues and solve the problems, within a very short period, and without completely burning out our team..."

When describing your situation, the above example is going to be a good *summary* that you can use to remind yourself of the example — at best. But it's by no means going to be what you actually say in the interview. It is non-descriptive, vague, and lacks any real substance. It's such a generic answer that the interviewer will inevitably follow up by asking,

What was the product? What was the company? Why did development stall? How big was the team? What was your position? What do you mean "on track?" When was this again?

When they ask these questions, you will end up re-telling the story again. And if you don't have the answers to these basic details, you're in big trouble.

Again, this does not mean that you need to give a much longer description. Too much irrelevant detail is redundant. There has to be a point to what you are saying and a reason for the details you are describing.

Remember, the main reason we add detail is to give the listener *context.*

The point is: **generic answers will give you generic results.**

Questionable Examples

There are some things that you just shouldn't talk about. Often we will get excited about an example because we have a good story behind it. Like how you described a time you faced pushback, but then end up describing the time you proved your boss wrong and rubbed it in his face. Or how you were drunk at a company event and learned a lesson about professionalism — but then unnecessarily including all of the suggestive details like the color and consistency of your vomit that evening.

Now some people might object with, *"But I don't want to hide my "true self." This is who I am, and I don't want to lie to the interviewer."*

What is your "true self?" Do you act the same in front of your spouse, your friends, children, and your boss? How about your parents? If you speak more than one language, do you speak and act the same way in both languages?

Most people would be hard-pressed to say yes; they absolutely put on the same face with everyone in their lives. Shakespeare said it best — *All the world's a stage.* It all goes back to context and situation. Your mother will probably never ask you to explain your decision-making process when you created a 3-month strategy for your sales team.

There's nothing wrong with this. Interviews are not a natural setting — but they're not an unnatural setting either.

What is a "natural" setting, anyway? Does it mean it's a situation where we would find ourselves in nature? That's a rarity all around. Or does it mean we are comfortable? I think we take it to mean the latter in most situations.

Here's the deal: Things become "natural" as we grow more comfortable with them. As we practice more and more, we become more comfortable. Thus, the key to having a "natural" conversation is to practice conversing.

We can open up different sides of ourselves, our hobbies, our personal lives, and so forth once we get to know people. But in a professional context, you have certain expectations of your coworkers and boss — raising the bar, transparency, communication. The values you have and seek for in a job. These are the aspects you should focus on.

You do not need to be best friends with your coworkers. In fact, approaching your job in this way can be risky, as it might shut down opportunities where you don't feel 100% comfortable speaking to someone you met in the interview process. It's very likely you won't get along with everyone, and that's ok. Once you hired, you can choose your friends and will likely gravitate towards certain people, as you do in life.

Going back to the main point — *you can be yourself without revealing every little detail and you can (and should) still act professionally.* Focus on the stories that are professional and appropriate throughout the interview process. Once you are in the company and get to know the team, then you can share your weird and wacky stories.

Blame and Ownership

When you are starting out in your career, you typically have a predefined set of tasks. When you screw up, you are responsible for your screw-up and have to figure it out. Sometimes it escalates to your manager, and they have to help. But usually, it's your problem.

As you move up in an organization, you become increasingly responsible for other people's problems. As a manager, when your teammate does something to upset a customer, you will likely have to get involved and help them apologize and handle the situation.

You take ownership for that mistake even though it wasn't your fault.

A word of caution when framing the situation/problem that arose. Even if you are telling a story about your first few months on the job, be careful not to lay blame on anyone. The point of any story is not whose "fault" it was, but rather, how YOU were involved in helping solve the problem.

Former Navy Seal and author Jocko Willink talks about this in his book, *Extreme Ownership.*[xvi] He points out that

99.9% of failure in the Navy Seals has nothing to do with physical skills or mental toughness.

"What makes a person fail as a leader is that they are not humble enough to accept responsibility for their mistakes…[…] Ego drive can be good and pushes people to do better. Where ego becomes the enemy is when it becomes too big. They can't take criticism, and they can't take ownership when mistakes happen, so they point fingers at other people. With ownership, you take control of your ego and take responsibility for your actions."

When you explain how you were involved and looked at things objectively, you gain brownie points. Especially if you were in a management position, I find the best way to talk about a problem is to use the word "we". That works well to show that you have a sense of responsibility that extends beyond yourself as well as a need to solve the problem.

We had an angry customer….and I did X.
We had a bottleneck in the sales process….and I did Y.
We had low team morale….So I did X.
We had a bad quarter and did not meet our sales quota….So I responded with X.

Now that you have defined the problem/situation, we can move on to define what tasks **you** were assigned and/or what your duty was.

But before we do, let's refine the *situation* in your STAR story.

PRACTICE

We are sticking with the question of "biggest achievement" for now but if you want to write about other examples (how you met a deadline, handled pressure, etc.) then go for it, but go back to the start of this chapter and start with the *brain dump.*

Now let's do the following:

1. Look at your notes. Start writing down everything you can remember about the situation in as much detail as possible. Use the Excel document that you made.
2. Use the *"Context is Key"* guide in this chapter to help list more details.
3. Ask yourself the question "why" at least five times for the situation until you cannot answer any longer. *Why did this situation happen? Why did I feel that way? Why was it an issue? Why did I have to take care of it? Why did x happen and not y?*
4. Now shorten it. Get your situation down to 1 minute or less. If you practice and your situation lasts more than 1 minute, take out any unnecessary filler words and make it more concise. I recommend using your phone timer or stopwatch to measure. Make sure you are rehearsing in a relaxed and comfortable pace -- it can be easy to rush.
5. Condense the situation to one sentence. This will make it easier for you to remember.
6. Now practice it out loud.

STAR EXAMPLE

"Describe a time when you had to influence a stakeholder."

S   During my time as a freelance translator my goal was to localize the website "Digital Garage" from English into Japanese. Before submitting to translation, we needed to decide the Japanese name. The global marketing team, as well as the Japanese marketing point of contact, wanted to go with the English name or direct translation. However, the English name or the direct translation could cause an issue in the Japanese market as it didn't translate very well.

T   I needed to convince the stakeholders why we should use a different name in the Japanese market. #1) Japanese people don't have an especially good impression of the word "Garage." Garage simply means a place where cars are parked, and unnecessary stuff is stored. #2) There is an advertising agency named "Digital Garage" in Japan. To avoid any misunderstanding or confusion, we needed to use the different name.

A   I made a suggestion to go with "Digital Workshop" based on my explanation of these three criteria in a group meeting with the marketing team. I gave them context which they previously didn't have with the language. Once they heard it from a Japanese person's perspective, the problem and solution were made clear through my suggestions.

R   They understood the points I raised and decided to

go with my idea. The launch of the website ran smoothly, and we did a post-launch analysis of what our customers on Twitter and Facebook were saying. Overall the brand received a very positive reception, and we never heard of any issues around the naming of the site.

CHAPTER 3

TASK

What was your specific duty or goal during the specific event/situation? What was your responsibility? What was at stake?

> *"Sometimes the first duty of intelligent men*
> *is the restatement of the obvious."*
> -George Orwell

Zoom In

Situation and task can connect almost seamlessly. If we think about the situation as describing the problem you encountered, we can think about the task as the *responsibility or duty* that you have. Now that you've been put into a certain situation, **what is the goal and what is your role in the situation?**

Zoom in and define this in simple terms.

Let's say your department is going through a series of layoffs during your time as a manager. The situation results in low morale and team spirit which lowers productivity. This is the situation. The task will be a definition of your responsibility you have in the situation.

"As a manager, it was my responsibility to boost morale and get everyone through this tough time." That's it. The task can start with one or two simple sentences stating what you were doing at the time.

The task will be a statement of what you have to do, or what you're supposed to, while the action or actions you define will be specific. *"My task as manager is to remain positive and help boost morale, and my actions to get there were X Y and Z."*

But that doesn't mean your task will be general — you can still quantify it. For example:

Situation: Advertising revenue was falling, and our advertisers were not renewing contracts.

Task: As an advertising account manager, my role was to increase advertising sales by 15% over the previous year.

In this case, you have a specific number, in other cases where you don't have a tangible number in the "task" you can make up for this in your description of the action and results.

Zoom Out

The importance of the task may not be self-evident, so we don't want to assume the interviewer implicitly understands how important this task was. We thus need to spell it out for them. *What is the significance of completing this task? What is at stake if you do not complete the task?*

Zoom out. Take a higher level perspective and explain the impact.

This doesn't mean you have to over-emphasize or blow up the situation. The importance of the task, like anything, can be relative to the situation. For example, if you are a web designer and are deciding on which two shades of blue to use for a button on a web page, this in itself may seem trivial or unimportant. But the site gets 10 million views monthly so if we choose the "less attractive" blue this could result in a very, very significant amount of people not clicking it, and possibly millions in lost revenue.

Stating the importance in terms of a specific monetary amount or at least a tangible outcome drives the point home. *"If we got this wrong we could lose X amount of dollars. That's what was at stake, and it was my responsibility to solve this."* Or in the case of the manager whose department is going through layoffs, it could be *"We just lost eight people in the department and the team was overworked, morale was low. If we lost another person, the situation could spiral out of control, and it could cause others to start resigning. It was my duty as a manager to boost morale and make sure this didn't happen."*

The point is that we need to both zoom in *and* zoom out. You are probably better at one of these than the other. Which one is it? Some people are process-driven and are great at remembering minute details. But they often fail to understand why they are doing something and don't grasp the bigger picture. If they did, perhaps they might take a completely different trajectory or challenge the status quo. Other people are great at understanding *why* something is being done and can see the vision or higher purpose. But they might fail to see the step-by-step process necessary to get there and thus miss important details or hold unreasonable expectations. Rarely do we find people that are balanced and extremely skilled in both areas. So we need to identify which side we lean towards, take the side we are weaker in and do our best to balance ourselves out.

Another way to look at "what's at stake" is asking yourself "what's the anticipated consequence?" What if you faced the problem and did nothing? If you just ignored it, what would have happened?

Trimming the Hedges

Just like in the *Situation,* there is a fine line between necessary details and redundancy. In the example of layoffs above, if you are responding to "tell me about a tough time where you showed leadership ability," the interviewer might not need to know everything about *why* the layoffs happened. They want to know what your role was at the time and what was at stake. If they feel the gravity of the situation and the importance of the tasks at hand, you've told a good story.

Here's another scenario. Imagine that your approach to boosting morale is to first schedule a meeting with the whole team. You gather your team and ask, *"Do you understand why these layoffs happened? What questions/ concerns do you have?"* If that is your approach as a manager in that particular situation, then you may very well need to mention it in your explanation of your action later on in your story.

Or maybe the interviewer had phrased the question differently: *"Why do you think it's difficult for people to change, and how have you faced this in the past?"* Your answer might pull on the same example but will be phrased differently.

"Simple answer: because people don't understand the why *behind things. For example, during company-wide layoffs, we experienced a massive decrease in productivity and an increase in people taking sick leave. It was my duty as manager to boost morale and get things back to normal. My first idea was to understand what people were feeling and listen to their perspectives. I took action and gathered everyone into a room. I quickly realized there was a lot of confusion about why the layoffs had happened. There was a miscommunication somewhere down the line. I immediately clarified the reasons which were X and Y. This taught me that often the biggest barrier to change is understanding* why *something happened, and getting people on the same page."*

Indeed, we can use the same example and the same situation to answer multiple questions!

There will be some details that are more relevant than others. Perhaps there were 3 or 4 actions you took in the above example that can all answer different questions.

This is one reason that we want to jot down as many details as possible in our brain dump. Often we've demonstrated a lot of different qualities in one example. Your greatest achievement may also include times that you showed leadership, thought outside the box, and hit a deadline.

We'll go over how to get the most out of this in the final chapter, but for now keep in mind that all of the details are important, and we will trim and shape different stories depending on the questions that are asked.

Ambiguity

In some instances, your task might not be straightforward. You might be thrown into a situation where you are not sure what you are supposed to do, and you're not exactly sure where your responsibility is or how far it can reach, but you do something anyway and figure it out. Sometimes there is no clear path and no clear data in hand.

That's ok. In this case, we can skip over the task and describe the process you took to come up with an action plan. We just have to frame it the right way.

Feelings and intuition often fall into this category. In reality, intuition isn't magic. It's built through years of experience. Often this is spoken about in parallel with the 10,000-hour rule, which states that to become an expert in something you need to have accumulated 10,000 hours of practice in that area.

If you've worked as a criminal investigator for 20 years, you have probably seen hundreds, maybe thousands, of different crime scenes. You have interrogated dozens of people and searched through thousands of files. When you find a "clue" sometimes you will just naturally follow it, not because of any hard evidence, but because you've been in the situation a million times before and you have a familiar sense. Can you objectively quantify this? Can you explain why you chose to do X and not Y in this situation? Maybe, maybe not.

But just saying "I had a feeling" or "based on years of experience" does not really make a good story, and it's certainly not convincing to an interviewer. The results you had might certainly be a testament that yes, you can do the job, but results are not enough. People want to know that you can replicate these results, the key is *showing them how*.

Let's say that you are a partnership manager for a software company. You are about to close a deal that will require your company to invest USD 5 million. You're having dinner with the client, and you get a strange vibe or feeling from them, like they're not telling you something. You brush it off but then it pops up in your head again after dinner. This is intangible, and you can't explain it to anyone, and there isn't a clear action to take. You think, *Are they going to screw me on this deal? What am I missing here?* You might start to doubt yourself and double check sales numbers or the contract or the terms of the deal. After going through every possibility, you're unable to find any huge reason to worry.

Unable to shake the feeling, you postpone the deal for one week.

Within that week the client announces their dismal quarterly earnings and decision to pull back on investments for many of their key products. The deal that once seemed great for both sides is now much less favorable, especially considering the upfront costs you would have to pay that are now based on a pretty shaky foundation. Happy you waited, you pull the plug on the deal.

How do you explain this intuition to an interviewer?

Just because we have a feeling or emotion that keeps popping up in our head doesn't mean we should act on it. If we did, then we wouldn't be much of a civilized society without a hint of self-control. I don't know about you, but that's not the kind of world I want to live in.

But sometimes you should act on feelings, even if you can't explain them. All good business leaders should be able to use data, numbers, and logic to make a decision. But they should also have good business judgment, which comes from *experience* -- not a spreadsheet.

If you're faced with a question that requires you to talk about making a judgment based on your intuition, or that you made with insufficient data, it's a great opportunity to showcase yourself. The key is to go back in time and pull apart everything that could have played a contributing factor.

"I was confident about the details of the partnership, and triple checked everything myself, and with my team. But there will always be surprises that pop up, which are not possible to predict, so I decided to trust my gut that something was not right. 5 million dollars was at stake here, and there was no harm in waiting an extra week, so we stalled the negotiation for several days. This proved to be the right decision because..."

In this case, your task as a leader is to make sure that you are making the right deals. You could say this explicitly, but in the story, it's woven implicitly and still gets the point across.

A follow-up question from the interviewer might be, *"What was it about the meeting that made you doubt them? Had they done something previously to justify this skepticism?"*

This is where you can chime in with extra details. Perhaps this was your first time working with this partner, so you were extra cautious about making this deal. Or perhaps it's simply your nature to fact check and triple check everything, and you make this part of your approach with all partners. Or perhaps it was a comment that the client made that made you think twice, which could be attributed to your high emotional intelligence (but don't flatter yourself too much). These are potentially details you could include in your initial description of the situation to make them, less feeling-based and more specific.

Analysis

Often before you know the tasks at hand, you need to do some analysis. You discover something. Or something is told or explained to you which drives you to take action.

A problem can arise from your analysis of tasks. This is where situation and task blends together, but don't get too bogged down with making a perfect structure. More importantly, we need to make sure to be clear about what the problem was, how we came to the realization, and providing context around that.

There are many ways the task can manifest. Here are a few examples:

#1 You are in charge of social media marketing at an advertising agency. That's the situation. Through your monthly reporting, you realize that Facebook engagement has decreased significantly. This is still part of the situation. Your job is to run social media and optimize campaigns, so you need to turn this negative number into a positive one. So, your job is to increase Facebook engagement. **That's your task.** From there, we would move on to action. There will be several actions you take to improve engagement — further analysis to determine the cause, changing creatives, switching budget allocation, and so on and so forth.

#2 Your boss will simply come and tell you. This is much more straightforward. *"Hey, we have an issue with this client who has been complaining about your communication style as too casual. We need to discuss professionalism on the job."* The problem has been thrust upon you, and your task has been assigned to you — figure out how to be a more professional communicator. To do so, you need to self-analyze and reflect.

#3 In other cases, you are thrown into the situation and have a short timeline to understand what is going on and figure out the tasks and actions that need to be taken.

For example, if you are working in a retail clothing store and suddenly you have one person that calls in sick, and then a swarm of 200 customers show up on the busiest day of the season, you better think of something quick.

But what is the task here? First, we'd have to start by really defining the problem. There were too many customers, and you were understaffed. What's at stake? This would result in poor customer service and lower sales because people don't want to stand in line and wait. Money and reputation are at stake. Your task is to figure out how to mitigate this, in whatever way you can. And then you have to spring into action.

What interviewers are looking for

Most interviewers are not well trained. They prepare a few questions they want to ask you and have an idea of what they want for the job, but they usually never write it down in full detail. They don't create a list of competencies for the job nor do they spend 3 hours with you to understand your background. You get one hour, two at most, and then maybe you meet some other people who also judge you based on their own criteria.

No wonder most interviews aren't a great indicator of on-the-job-performance.

The problem here is that a good interviewer is as important as the candidate who prepares for the interview. Both sides have to extract meaningful information from one another to understand each other, or else they rely on random hiring practices, their gut feelings, or a first impression they formed within the first 5 seconds of shaking your hand. Maybe your handshake was a little bit too firm, or maybe your hand was a little bit cold. They've done studies showing that shaking a cold hand lowers the positive impression you have about somebody compared to having a warmer hand. We turn a cold shoulder or warm up to them. Are people so fallible? Absolutely.

There is no magical solution. We cannot control all of these different external factors nor does it make sense to try.

Let's focus on what we can control.

<u>We can control what we say and the impression we give and the picture we paint. We have artistic freedom to include what we want and to take out other pieces.</u>

Interviews will often take the form of going through your entire work history in chronological order, starting from the start of your career to the present moment. If you are lucky, they will spend the time to go through each job position in detail and ask you questions like, "How was your performance in this job? Why did you leave? What was your biggest accomplishment?"

Other times they will not take the time to go through your entire work history in this much detail, which can be your downfall. The problem is that you never know what they are thinking and because the competencies for the job you are applying for are not 100% crystal clear, you want to divulge a lot of information here.

For interviewers to see the *real* you, in the context of your job, your achievements, your weaknesses, they will need to hear the stories that shaped you. It's *your* job to do that.

If you do not share those stories, then you risk missing some key details that could shift an interviewer's perception and change their understanding for the better.

For example, imagine you are describing your two years working as a sales manager at your previous job. You describe your sales achievements, say, USD 800,000 in sales your first year. The interviewer does not seem impressed because at his company a good sales guy brings in on average USD 4 million. You could describe how this increased over two years, but you miss a key chance to show how big of an impact this has.

The key here is to explain how your sales compared to the *previous* year. When you joined, the top sales guy was bringing in USD 200,000. You came in and quadrupled that. Now that's an achievement. Showing how your achievement is great relative to the company's expected performance is key.

Now they will want to know, *how did you do it?* This all comes down to adding a lot of context and detail to your story.

Often when people are asked, *"what was your biggest achievement?"* they will start off with a very short explanation and summary of what happened and the result.

"In my previous company, I hired two sales people and promoted them within one year. They ended up becoming top performers very quickly and went off to start new departments in the organization. It was exciting to see them grow and I'm personally motivated to see the development of others around me."

There's nothing wrong with this approach. As long as you have prepared a very detailed STAR story and done a deep dive during your preparation, then you'll be able to answer the upcoming firestorm of questions that will inevitably transpire.

The interviewer will never be satisfied with this answer. They might be intrigued, but they will inevitably want to hear more. They will follow up with questions like:

Great, tell me more.
How did you find them?
What was your management style?
How did you train them?
What was the criteria to promote them?

And so on. Of course, if you have context into exactly the type of person the interviewer is looking for, you can elaborate with a more detailed STAR story from the start.

So, with that in mind, we have two approaches here.

#1 You have a lot of context about the job you are interviewing for and understand the job description and business very well. In that case, you can tailor your situation, task, action, and results to the job to come up with relevant stories.

#2 You do not have a lot of context about the job you are interviewing for and still trying to understand the key pieces and requirements. In that case, when answering with your STAR story, you should start with a general summary of the story similar to the one mentioned above. Based on your summary, the interviewer will ask follow up questions, and then you can launch into more granular details of your STAR story.

Either way, the brain dump exercise and practicing key points about your STAR story are going to play out. They will just do so in slightly different ways.

Let's practice:

Tack on and define the task, tying it all in together.

1. Starting with your situation from the last chapter, describe what task you had to perform.
2. Make sure to include your duty, what was at stake, and take both a deep-dive and high-level view.
3. Start writing down everything you can remember about the task in as much detail as possible. Use the Excel document that you made to fill out details under "task."
4. Ask yourself these questions and include in your detailed list to help spurt more ideas. *How did I feel during the situation? What was at stake? Was there any ambiguity or was my responsibility clearly defined? How did I know what tasks were my duty vs someone else's? Is this an appropriate example? Can I quantify my task with numbers?*
5. Now come up with a 1-2 sentence description of your task. Get your task down to a few seconds. If it goes over 1 minute, take out any unnecessary filler words and make it more concise.
6. Practice it out loud.

STAR EXAMPLE

Describe a time when an idea you believed in was met with resistance. How did you handle it?

S   After graduating university I started work as an English teacher in China. My students were mainly businessmen and young adults who wanted to brush up on their English for their jobs. As teachers we were provided textbooks and workbooks, however, they were really out of date. While we never received complaints from the students, I knew that there was better material out there.

T   I wanted to convince my boss that we should find better textbooks. By keeping these older textbooks, I felt it slowed down the students and frustrated the teachers. Efficiency was at stake.

A   My plan was simple. Over a span of two weeks I did extensive research on other textbook options and came up with the following plan which I presented to my boss:

     1. After researching various options, I came up with the three textbooks which had great reviews and were recommended by teachers in some of the top foreign language institutes around the world. I purchased the books and showed them to my boss.

     2. I then presented a plan to make it happen. We could gradually replace all of the 200 work books for a discounted price of $1,500. We

could donate the rest of the books to local schools in China.

R   He shot down my idea almost immediately, citing the fact that they had a standardized textbook policy across all of the English schools they owned in China. Changing one book required various approvals from management and would take several months. I told him that it was better to do it later than never, however, I ultimately failed to convince him as he didn't seem to be keen to push through all of the bureaucracy required.

This was frustrating at the time, and I didn't take time to consider alternatives. For me, not having the textbooks was a "make it or break it" situation, and I felt that denying students books was unjust.

After further discussion, my boss was still supportive, and we came up with a separate plan to make the current classes more engaging for the students with supplementary materials. I realized that there were other ways to make the student lessons more engaging through the additional material, which didn't need approvals, — videos, music, articles, and other activities. My initial focus on textbooks created a blind spot, and I missed other obvious options. I learned that I shouldn't hold on to my opinions too dearly and that there are usually alternative solutions.

CHAPTER 4:

ACTION

Describe the actions you took to address the situation. It's important to define how you were specifically involved. Why did you take those actions? What did you do and what did your team do?

"Action expresses priorities."
-Ghandi

Decision Making Process

The task is your duty in your defined role, whether that was the CEO or a marketing manager. You might have a problem in front of you, fully understand your place in the situation, and know what problem you have to fix. But before you can take the logical next action steps, you need to clarify *what on earth your thought process was.*

Between the task and the action, you decide what to do and why to do it. Before you can take action, there is something that drives you to take a step forward. Sometimes that step is instinctual and stems from years of facing similar problems, but often you have to sit down and map things out.

Here's what to do next:

- Using your greatest achievement example, describe the logical steps you took to decide on what actions to take.
- Explain the reasons behind your decisions.
- Was this a short-term, mid-term, or long-term solution?
- Was anyone else involved in the decision-making process?

Now that you have outlined your decision-making process, you can describe what actions you took based on those decisions.

Where to Start

The action is the most important part of a STAR story. It's also likely to be the bulk of your answer and require the most detail.

If your action description is vague or if you can't explain why you took a certain action, it will detract from your ability to explain your point and influence the interviewer. In the worst case, the details of the situation and task are fuzzy, and the result was a failure, but your actions and reasons for taking those actions were crystal clear. The interviewer will then have a good idea of the type of actions you took as at least some sort of predictor of future behavior.

One of the biggest missteps I see people make is mixing up their actions and the actions of others. The distinction might seem apparent, but the lines can often be blurry in a team setting.

Be careful as you might get an interviewer like Elon Musk, who is well-known for making a clear distinction whether you did what you said you did.[xvii] His technique is to ask very, very minute details about the problems you solved. His logic is that if you solved the problem, you'd be pretty familiar with all of the specifics.

If you had a team of 5 people and *you* decided to do X, then who took the actions? Did you, or your team or both? How were the actions split up and what role did you play? Were you playing the role of a delegator? Or were you on the front lines taking action yourself? Again, there is no right or wrong answer, but we need to make this distinction.

The easiest way to do this is to use your pronouns properly. When you say "I did x" it should mean that you took that action by yourself. If other people were involved, then be specific.

"As a member of the event planning team, I was put in charge of finding sponsors for our yearly summer event. The first step was to survey managers in our company to ask if they had any suggested sponsors. I delegated this list-making task to our intern at the time. After she had made a list, I personally called all of the potential sponsors and gave them the pitch for our event..."

You might be wondering why it's necessary to mention the intern in this situation, as it seems like an unnecessary or trivial piece to your story. First, you are being honest. Second and more importantly, you are trying to paint an accurate picture of **your skills,** so it's important to represent the actions that you took. That way there are no miscommunications down the line. Perhaps you are very good at executing on a sales pitch or strategy, but you dislike doing research online or are very bad with Microsoft Excel. If the job you are applying for requires extensive online research and data entry, it's important to clarify this early on. If it wasn't a big part of your previous job, is it something you are willing to do or not?

When I was interviewing to become a recruiter, I was asked the obvious question that always came up for new grads, *"do you have any sales experience?"* Fortunately, I had worked part-time as a door-to-door knife salesman. This required me to call random people from the phone book and spend all summer in the Texas-heat (I'm talkin' "Howdy partner"-heat) knocking on doors trying to sell people $2,000 knife sets that they didn't need.

While I wouldn't be selling any knives in my recruitment job, I was able to draw parallels between transferable skills in my sales job (perseverance, tenacity, people skills) to what was required in recruitment -- and the interviewers dug it. I was hired. After joining the company, I realized that indeed the core sales and people skills were not all too different.

There are many reasons that people fail in their new jobs and quit within the first few months. One of the common reasons that I often hear (other than "my boss sucks") is the discrepancy between their job duties and what was described in the interview. Within a few weeks or months of joining, someone who accepted a marketing position might realize it is more of a sales job. They feel overwhelmed, or they don't enjoy what they are doing.

This might not have been accurately described in the job interview, and it's easy to blame the company or hiring manager for not giving us a "fair shot" or being transparent.

While this explanation is possible, let's not play the victim here.

More likely than not, people have not have taken the time to really, accurately describe what they were doing in their previous jobs. They get excited about taking a job offer and jump head first into something without doing their due diligence.

They may not have provided enough information to the interviewer and just "sold themselves" by saying what they needed to say to impress the interviewer. The interviewer is human and susceptible to making emotional decisions just like the rest of us, so they could have hired you with the "faith" that things would work out, or believed your sales pitch that might have slightly stretched the truth.

Now, here is an important distinction between fictitious storytelling and STAR stories. Your STAR stories are not fake. They happened. So, anything you do to fudge the truth will probably come back to bite you.

There is nothing wrong with trying to impress an interviewer, but we have to be honest with ourselves when it comes to our job experience. When you have only managed two people in your career and are applying for a job where you need to manage six people, three of whom are located overseas, there will be new challenges.

It's easy to get caught up in the excitement — "Yes, I can do it." Most people say this without thinking. But really, many of the times they *can't* do it.

You've never done it, but you want to. What's your plan? If you don't have a plan to get there and have no job experience in that area, you should slow down for a second and consider whether or not this position is the right move.

I find the best approach is to mix humility with enthusiasm, and then sprinkle in a bit of realism. *"It will probably take me 3-6 months to get the hang of the company's system. I'm willing to work hard and learn from others to get there. But once I get comfortable with the new system, I think I'll be able to excel in the role."*

I don't like the advice "underpromise and overdeliver" because you're basically saying that potential employers shouldn't expect much from you. You can still set high expectations but be realistic throughout the process. Set the expectations fairly high but not *too* high.

Another example would be putting down "proficient in Microsoft Excel" and then describing all of the different reports that you created using the software, failing to mention that you had another teammate who was constantly re-checking and fixing your work. If you were hired and then the job did require quite a bit of Excel, you'll either have to learn it fast, or you'll be in for a shock when you don't have the same support system as your previous job.

Remember — you and only you are responsible for doing due diligence before accepting a job offer.

The 4 Elements of the Action Point

#1: How? How did you come up with the idea to take this specific action? Did you have to speak to any people? Did you have to analyze any data? Did you have any similar experiences in the past? There were certainly different actions you could have taken, so list out all of your options.

#2: Why? Why did you choose to take that specific action, out of all of the other possibilities? What was at stake if you were wrong? What if you didn't have all of the information in point #1, do you think you would have chosen a different action?

#3: What? What did you do? How long did it take you? Were there any hiccups? Did you need permission? How did you feel?

#4: Who? Was anyone else involved in taking action, or was it only you? Make the distinction between "I" and "we." People prefer to hear about what you did specifically.

Let's illustrate with an example:

Situation and task: I was working as an advertising sales manager at TrezPress, an online business which publishes reviews of high tech gadgets. At the start of the second quarter my team, six people, including myself, made no revenue for the first two months. Our monthly target was 100k USD monthly. This really lowered team morale and caused a spiral of negativity. (Task) As a team manager, it was my goal to boost morale, motivate staff and get our sales target back up.

Action (split up into 4 points):

#1: How? I first needed to assess why this was happening. This was my first job as a manager, and I hadn't been in a similar situation before, so I asked our director for guidance. He suggested I get to the root of the problem.

#2: Why? Taking his advice, I spoke to my whole team about what they were feeling and what had been going on the past two months. The consensus was that morale had lowered because of two big sales deals that we lost at the start of the quarter. Everyone had a bad start.

#3: What? Realizing that we still had what it took, but simply had a bad a start, I decided to try out various initiatives to give the team a boost. First, I created a team incentive trip if we hit our 2-week target. Second, I became more hands-on in the day-to-day sales activities, and attended five sales meetings each week, rotating with each team member. And lastly, I re-assessed our client portfolio to focus on the top 20% of clients that were generating 80% of the revenue.

#4: Who? I took the lead on all three action points and was the key driver for these initiatives. For the team incentive, one of our more experienced team members contributed a lot at the desk while I was away. I was lucky to have such a positive teammate on board during tough times.

Result: The team hit their target over two weeks, winning the incentive which was a quick boost to morale. This started a positive spiral. I helped close one deal during my tag-along meetings, and after the reassessment of the portfolio, the team was more focused. Within six weeks we had made up our losses and achieved 85% of our target for the quarter. While it was not 100%, we came from the bottom to the top in a relatively short amount of time, and it's an achievement I'm proud of.

Using numbers. No, not math.

Elon Musk famously has a rule to speed up decision making. Knowing that we will never have 100% of the information we need to make a decision, once he has 70% of the information necessary, he will pull the trigger.

Not all decisions can be made with data. We explored this before when we discussed ambiguity and using our gut feelings. Using numbers does not mean that you were running complex equations, nor do you need to do any hard-core math. "Back of the napkin" math will suffice.

The purpose is to illustrate better the methodology and scope of what you were doing. This means that you don't have to convert everything into percentages — no need to bog yourself down. The most effective and often the most difficult point is...Simply **having** the numbers. That's it.

Again, I am not asking you to do any math. No rocket science here and no need to pull out your TI-84 and start graphing.

The purpose of including numbers and quantifying your storytelling is to give the listener context and an understanding of the scope of what you have done, which will help in assessing the similarities and differences between your previous work and the job you are interviewing for.

There is no reason for us to keep numbers and percentages in our working memory when it has been weeks, months, and years since we saw them. And nobody is expecting you to. This is exactly why you need to go back, dig through papers, look at old emails and reports, ask colleagues, and do whatever else you need to do to find the basic information. As a side note, you'll want to have some of these figures already on your resume. And of course, you'll be expected to talk about them.

If you are describing how you administered a survey to your customers as part of a marketing campaign, it's enough to say *"we conducted a survey asking people if they would be interested in our new CRM product. We sent the survey to 200 people, and about 80 responded positively, 20 negatively."*

You don't need to include percentages for no reason unless they somehow relate to the result which you will describe later. There's no need to say *"we surveyed 200 people and 40% of them came back with a positive response and 20% with a negative response."* You can just say the actual numbers.

When you are digging through your experiences to find relevant details for your biggest accomplishment and other topics, here are other numbers and figures you should be looking up:

- What was the size of your company in terms of revenue? Was it profitable?
- How many people did your company have? Your department? How many of them were local and how many were overseas? Were some of them contractors? Full time?
- How much market share did your company or product have? What percentage, roughly?
- How big was your marketing budget for X project?
- What was your sales or business development target?
- What costs and expenses did your business or position incur?
- If you were in a general management position, what was the profit and loss? How did this increase or decrease over time? What factors influenced this?
- If you are in marketing, how much of your work was online vs offline?
- What was the time frame it took you to achieve X action?
- How did you spend your time in your job? 20% of administrative work and 80% on sales? Where was the majority of your time going?
- How many customers did you have? Clients? Paying customers? Free customers? Subscribers?

These questions are starting points that you should be able to answer. They are not complicated numbers but finding them might take some time. Also, they should help stir your memory for any other critical pieces and additions to your overall STAR story.

Every Story has a Premise

Right and wrong are relative. Everyone has different principles in life and the important question is not whether or not someone agrees with you, the question is *whether or not your actions are consistent with your principles*. And whether or not you have made that clear in your story. If you haven't then your story won't make sense and it will be confusing to readers and listeners.

Let's say that it's 1999 and you're an executive working at Yahoo. Your fundamental philosophy is that you should never sacrifice long-term growth for short-term profits.

You then share an example about a huge achievement where you closed a string of partnership deals with ten startup companies. This won your company a lot of money, and you got a promotion and the respect of your colleagues. But this was before the dot-com bubble exploded, and you knew that these companies were highly overvalued, being propped up by hopeful investors. You knew this, but most people didn't. The short-term revenue was great, but you were sure it was not sustainable and would eventually implode (which it did). You closed the deals anyway.

This action was fundamentally contradictory to your core philosophy, and if sharing this example, it's important you explain what happens next.

Were you along for a short ride? Did you cash out and leave after the bubble popped? Or did you end up staying at Yahoo, facing up to the plummet of share value after the bubble exploded with a commitment to creating a more transparent and long-term strategy for your business?

Your answer and how you responded in this situation will show the interviewer what actions you have taken, and they will take these actions as an indication of your core philosophy. If your core belief is different from what your actions show, then you will need to explicitly reveal your core philosophy and explain why you didn't act in line with your beliefs. This begs the question — what really is your core philosophy? Has it changed over time?

The first step is being crystal clear about your principles. Writing down principles is not something people do often, but it can be really helpful for life in general and guide your decisions more consistently. And in particular, for an interview, it will be easier to describe your experiences in the lens of your beliefs about how the world works.

Employers want to know how you act and behave in certain situations. Part of this is knowing what your beliefs are. Do you think it's ok to cut corners sometimes? Is it ok to make decisions without 100% of the data? Would you rather launch a decent product in time for the deadline, or miss the deadline and have a perfect product? How do you make these decisions, and what beliefs drive you?

There is no right or wrong answer. The point is that you just need to be clear on your principles.

Perhaps the situation is rather complex, and you need to explain how it does, in fact, stay consistent with your core philosophies. If it doesn't, then there will be a question mark about your logic and how, if at all, the employer can depend on you. What and how would you act in that situation if it were to arise again?

The conclusion the employer will make is that you are going to act the same way in a similar situation — after all, this is *behavioral interviewing*, so they are looking at your past behaviors to predict future outcomes. Unless you give them a reason to believe otherwise.

The easy way to test your philosophy against your actions is to ask yourself, *"why did I take this action?"* If the situation were slightly different, would you have taken a different action? Was there any inherent bias that you had? Did something someone did or say influence you? Did you get a spark of inspiration somewhere? Were you deterred by something you read, heard, saw or experienced?

When you can pinpoint why you took a certain action, you can then bring it back and ask what you would do in a similar situation.

Let's say you see a colleague acting condescendingly towards a new employee who recently joined the team. What do you do? Are you going to call him out on it in front of other people, and publicly address the issue to prove a point? Or are you going to pull him aside immediately and give him negative feedback privately? What would *you* do?

At the core, you might believe that negative feedback

should always be given privately, in which case you would go with the latter option. You would have examples that demonstrate this. On the other hand, if you think that it's important to deter this sort of behavior on a company-wide level and thus address someone publicly, then you would choose the former.

Image the interviewer asks you about your philosophy on negative feedback, and you answer that it should be given privately. He then asks for examples, but all you can think of are times when you have given it publicly. You see there; there's obviously a disconnect between your actions and beliefs. That's what I mean.

Now think back. Are there any times when your beliefs were inconsistent with your actions? Why was that? Be honest. Write them down. You might find hidden weaknesses which you can improve on. You can talk about those, as long as you are self-reflective and can address them constructively with "I need to improve x and y."

The good news is that if all your actions don't match up with your beliefs, then congratulations, you are human. However, more often than not you'll find that you tend to do certain things a certain way. Nailing down concretely what your principles are is the key to presenting your ideas concisely and expressing yourself boldly.

Strategy Vs. Tactics

Tactics are simply short-term actions that you take to get things done. Strategy refers to longer-term direction and planning. You need tactics to execute strategy. And without a strategy, tactics have no purpose and no real "why." Did you take a strategic or tactical approach? How do you know? Why is it important for employers?

Typically at the beginning of our career, we are assigned certain tasks without much decision making power. Working as a waiter at a restaurant we might rhetorically ask the question, *"Why do I have to clean the bathroom three times a day?"* The reason for cleaning the bathroom seems self-evident — they have to stay clean because there are safety inspections, customers will complain if they're dirty, and dirty bathrooms are gross. Beyond this, it's doubtful that we are thinking about the longer term "bathroom-cleaning strategy" within the scope of the overall business. We don't need to. Our task is clearly defined, and our responsibility doesn't extend beyond waiting tables and cleaning bathrooms.

If you are the manager of the restaurant, your goal for the year might be to get a 10/10 customer service rating. You know this will create more publicity for the restaurant, resulting in more sales and put you up for a promotion to regional manager. The standard for others restaurant chains is to clean the bathrooms once a day. But because you want to ensure the 10/10 customer service rating, you make 3-a-day cleanings mandatory as part of your overarching strategy. The employees below you may or may not know this, as they are simply responsible for executing the strategy's tactics— cleaning the bathrooms.

A good manager, of course, will make clear the purpose and the "why" of doing certain things. They will lay out the customer service strategy and explain to the employees why they have to clean the bathrooms three times a day. They will provide some vision of a greater goal and hopefully an incentive — monetary or otherwise, that the employees can look forward to.

Typically we are more tactical early on in our careers when we are learning the ropes. We have the strategy set down by a great leader, manager or CEO. We then execute their strategy. While they focus on the bigger picture, we focus on the little details and executing the plan to fulfill the strategy and achieve the goals.

As we gain more experience we come to understand *why* we do certain things, and that there are different ways to accomplish goals. We get a better sense of how to achieve our goals and might start to become more involved in making strategy ourselves. We might become critical of the strategy because we think we could have come up with something better. Sometimes we are right; sometimes we are wrong. Things are easier to criticize when we have the benefit of hindsight.

In an ideal world, we have people who can see both the vision and are hands-on in the day to day tactics. But in reality, this is not practical because the CEO is not going to check every little detail of a 200 person marketing team. Similarly, the marketing manager will not necessarily have the full picture in a company to decide on what product lines to cut. It's tempting to make big generalizations about what a good CEO should and shouldn't be, or what a good marketing manager should or shouldn't be. There is no absolute 'good' or 'bad' but we can speak regarding specific actions and results.

Here's what I mean: You can be a really good tactician and a poor strategist, and vice versa. In the context of answering an interview question with a good story, the interviewer will be looking for clues on both. You need to watch out for both. Often showing both sides can be beneficial.

For example:

If the position is entry level and requires data-entry and secretary work, then strategic planning might not be a big factor. But what if it was? What if you could demonstrate how strategic you were as an executive secretary, planning months in advance? This might set you apart from others who simply emphasize their organizational skills or ability to multi-task. Similarly, if you are interviewing for a senior sales management position, your storytelling ability and charisma to lead a tough sales team might be valued. But if you're not willing to get into the nitty-gritty details to identify specific sales problems or go to meet clients with your team, then are you really a good leader?

Typically when someone is very "tactical" people take this to be synonymous with being "hands-on." Depending on your job, there is a time and place for this.

For example, let's say you started your career in digital marketing for a company where you ran digital advertising campaigns. This required daily keyword planning, research on google trends, and optimizing campaigns. You have little say into the types of marketing the company was doing or how much they were spending on online marketing. Eventually, you become closer to the rest of the marketing team and begin to understand what kind of marketing initiatives they are running. You learn about social media marketing and quickly raise your hand to take on extra responsibilities. One day your marketing manager is off work, and you fill in for her during a management meeting, where you contribute your ideas to the current marketing strategy.

Quickly, your scope increases. You are starting to move from purely tactical operations to influencing strategy.

It would be a very big stretch to say that your time as a hands-on digital marketing specialist was pointless, or that if you had the opportunity, it would have been better to start out in a more senior position if you had the chance. This logic doesn't stand because, in order to set down a strategy that makes sense, you'll need to know the internal workings — the tactics.

As you learn how to crawl, you first look at your hands in front of you. One by one.

As you learn how to walk, you look at your feet marching one in front of the other.

Eventually, you learn how to run. Now you can see far out into the distance.

Impact Words

Actions are a big deal. It's easy to undervalue how big our actions were as they tend to fade with time. The point is that we want to stir up some of those same emotions we had during the time of the action. There are certain words we can use to make our actions sound more impactful. Simply, action verbs. You can check the free PDF mentioned at the start of the book for links to an extensive list of action verbs.

When you are writing an essay, then you have the benefit of having a list of words that you can use and pepper into your writing. When you are verbally telling a story, you have to go with the flow. Don't think too much about wording and let your story itself unravel. Of course, you can prepare words you might want to use beforehand.

This shouldn't turn into a vocabulary lesson, and you don't want to be looking up complicated words to try and make you sound smart. It will have the opposite effect. Rather, you want to ensure that the meaning behind what you are trying to say is accurately described. If during your STAR preparation (practicing in front of the mirror) you are trying to convey an emotion or idea and feel there is something missing, then that's the time to look up a word or synonym. Check out thesaurus.com

Too much pepper will make you sneeze. More importantly, you don't want to turn into an alliteration or onomatopoeia machine.

"I defined, designed, and then delegated the project. We

distributed resources and delivered results, resulting in double-digit growth."

If you could pull off this sort of poetic alliteration in your storytelling then I think your interviewer would be rather impressed. But I don't recommend it. You could use alliteration perhaps once in a story to give it some extra horsepower, alongside the "rule of 3's," for a powerful punch. Use it sparingly.

Practice:

Now let's tack on the action.

1. Using your situation and task from the last chapter, describe what action or actions you had to perform. What were your options?
2. Why did you choose X action? Was there any analysis involved? Were any other people involved in the action-taking?
3. Start writing down everything you can remember about the action in as much detail as possible. Use the Excel document that you made to fill out under "action."
4. Be specific about what **you** did and what other people did. We want to make sure your actions stand out in this example. What you did and what you didn't do.
5. Now come up with a 5-6 sentence description of your action. Get your action down to a few seconds verbally. If it goes over 1 minute, take out any unnecessary filler words and make it more concise.
6. Practice it out loud.

STAR EXAMPLE

S   During my last quarter of school, I completed an internship at Memorial Hospital in the Health Information Management department. I was the first and only intern the department had ever had, and they decided they wanted to continue with an official internship program.

T   To successfully launch this program, my supervisor asked me to create and administer a training curriculum for the new, incoming interns.

A   To complete this task, first, I outlined all the procedures the new interns would need to learn about like HIPAA standards, how to operate the 10-line phone system, and how to use the health record index and storage system. Next, I created a three-day training agenda covering these topics. Finally, I facilitated it to four new interns.

R   The training was a huge success. On a survey completed after the training, all four interns rated the program an 8 out of 10 in the areas of usefulness and creativity. It wasn't a 10 out of 10. Looking back, since I was the only intern I wasn't able to get feedback about my plan from other interns, but I could have worked a bit closer with the department to gauge their feedback before launching.

CHAPTER 5:

RESULTS

Describe the outcome of the actions you took. What impact did this have? Speak in terms of tangible outcomes tied to numbers and people. What did you learn?

"People love chopping wood. In this activity one immediately sees results."
-Albert Einstein

What was the impact?

You've gone through all the work of digging and writing down the details of past stories. Fantastic. Now you have to convince someone that your actions actually had an impact. And you have to show them what that impact was.

Many people tend to retreat into vague statements like "it was a success, and we achieved our goal." They stop there assuming that because they have specified the action, simply stating if the result was successful or not successful will suffice. But as you know by now, we need to be a little bit more specific.

Impact is relative. Getting your first ten customers is a success if that's the goal. This might pale in comparison to getting your 1 millionth customer, but that's ok. Don't fall prey to comparing everything or else you will go crazy. We can never be perfect, but we can strive for excellence. There will always be someone better than us. If we have a 1m USD business, someone out there is doing a 10m USD business. If we have a 10m USD business someone is out there doing a 100m USD business. And so on. It's never enough.

There will be times when you do better or worse, and there will always be people who seem to be achieving bigger things. That's life. As long as we are learning and growing, then we are doing the best that we can do.

It's important to explain the impact in relative terms to the situation. This goes back to "what was at stake?"

I was a girl scout, and my mom paid $200 upfront to purchase Girl Scout cookies that I needed to sell as part of an annual fundraiser. My goal was to sell all 200 boxes of cookies — but there was one problem - it was raining heavily the entire weekend. If I didn't sell the cookies, then my mom would be mad, and I would not get my Red Ribbon Girl Scout badge. We couldn't set up our booth in front of the store as planned. I was responsible for thinking of a plan B.

I brainstormed all of the indoor locations that we could set up. I started writing down a bunch of places. The store, church, DMV, movie theaters, retirement communities, the doctor, the library. This had never been done before, so I was taking a risk.

My Girl Scout group was made up of six people, so I decided that we could make three small groups and pick three locations. I delegated responsibilities. For two days we set up at the library, movie theater, and church. The church was logical because it would be busy on Sunday. I chose the movie theater because Spider-Man had just come out and it would be a busy weekend, and it was raining, pushing people toward indoor activities. And the library because more people will be inside on the rainy weekend.

We sold all 200 boxes of cookies — it worked! My mom and the team were very happy that we could sell the cookies. I later suggested to the Girl Scout Troop leader that we should start selling cookies at these places in the future, and our success served as a good template for other troops. She agreed that diversifying locations could help bring in more revenue, which was money we could then use for a big trip during the year. I believe that a little bit of creativity, while risky, went a long way to impact the direction of the Girl Scouts that year.

How to be "Commercial"

Describing your results is great. My goal was x, I analyzed z, I did y and achieved my goal of x. Simply stating the result, in any amount of detail, is not enough. The explanation has to come from a place of commercialism.

The idea of being "commercial" means that you fundamentally understand how a business works. You understand how it makes money, what the levers of the business are, and know how to make good judgments based on these factors. It doesn't matter what your profession is, you can develop a commercial mindset.

It's understanding the "why" and the gears in the machine. You can go for months and years working at a company but not understand how it operates. Where is the money coming from? What are the costs? How much is the business growing? What are the market trends?

These are questions you may not need to ask within your job. They may not seem to be directly relevant or important to your day to day operations. At most, they are interesting topics of conversation. But in reality, having a commercial mind and being able to answer questions commercially is very important.

Commercialism is something that might come naturally to some people — maybe they can smell the money, or they are born problem solvers. They need to understand how something works. It doesn't matter if you are one of 500 customer service representatives at a call center. You understand the business inside and out even though that might not be part of your job description. But for most people, commercialism will come with time. It will be fostered by working with a strong manager/leader and taking a proactive approach to constantly improve yourself.

Notice that I am emphasizing the "impact" and not using the world result. Results can be simple — the ROI, the number of users acquired, and the sales revenue. Of course, we need to state a tangible result, numerically if possible.

But I want you to start thinking about *impact* as a more commercial word. It can manifest in many ways, including the following:

- An understanding of the end product your business is selling.
- Understanding how your company makes money and the costs associated with that
- Knowing who your customers are.
- An interest in business and an understanding of the wider environment in which the business operates in.
- Understanding what category your business fits in, the overall market, and market trends.

Taking a commercial approach to your storytelling should manifest throughout your story. If you can answer "why" you did something, then you are on the right track. A lot of the macro/micro environment that we discussed in the situation chapter relates to this.

Performance

In reference to the result and impact of that result, here are several commercial questions that you can ask yourself.

How did your performance compare to the previous year's performance?

You can talk about achieving X and Y, but it's hard for the listener to grasp what this means without understanding the previous years. If you achieved 120% above your target for the past 3 years and are talking about achieving 100% in your third year, then this is actually a decrease in your performance. What happened? Were the targets higher, were there other factors that influenced this? A savvy interviewer will likely dig deeper in your performance and ask you "Is that a good result? How does it compare?"

How did your performance compare to your peers?

No need to brag here, but if you did 200% better than the rest of your peers and are an A player, then you should make that very clear. If you were in the top 10% of performers in your company, then you should make it clear. If this number changed over time, explain it. Showing a trajectory of positive growth and improvement can help. Even if you did not achieve your target or hit your goal, if you constantly improved every quarter for 2 years, then that means you are growing.

How did your performance compare to the original plan?

Every company has a goal or plans they set forward. Whether it's extremely specific, like 3-month targets based on a dozen measurable actions, or a single, straightforward goal like "achieve X in sales" or "launch this product by X time" or "increase customer satisfaction by X percent." What was your result compared to the plan that was set forward?

How does it compare to the industry?

This might be more difficult for you to answer without the data, but it can be extremely valuable for the interviewer to know. It shows a strong sense of commercialism if you can compare yourself across industry standards. It also serves as a good benchmark to assess your own value. For example, if you're the only person in the entire software industry to have made a deal with X company, then that's quite impressive. It's much more impressive than saying "I closed a big deal." You can do a bit of digging to find this information. So let's say that you want to know the average sales cycle within your industry. There are three ways to find out:

1) Ask experts offline. You can contact people in your network or that have worked in your industry. Usually, if the information is not extremely sensitive, they are willing to share. If the information is sensitive, you can always ask for ballpark figures.
2) Ask online. You can post your question on forums like Yahoo or Quora, and there is usually someone who is willing to share their expertise.
3) Research online. You can look up information on Crunchbase.com for public information. Also check quarterly earnings reports for potentially more detailed breakdowns.

The Million Dollar Question: Did you make or save the company money?

Interviewers are willing to hire you because they think you have the skills to do a job. If your job requires a repetitive task then it is likely to be replaced by a machine in the near future. Now more than ever you are faced with a very important question.

What value are you adding?

It might seem painfully cliché or overused. It is. But it's still important.

Either way, if you are in a "job" you perform actions that ultimately add to the growth of a company. If you can understand and articulate how you did this, then it means that you have a commercial understanding of the business. And while some companies truly love to see people grow and flourish, and make a fun environment that provides meaningful work — people are ultimately expendable. Unless they are solving a problem, and that problem is always somehow linked to making or saving money. *That* is how companies define value.

If you are a CFO, you could be saving the company millions through your corporate structuring and astute tax savings methods. If you are a great salesperson, you could be making the company millions in revenue and fueling growth. This is money the company can use to hire more people and build more stuff.

You might understand this conceptually, but the biggest challenge for many people is linking their tasks and actions to a monetary result. Often they aren't given that information or are not incentivized to think about it -- at least not until they are in more senior roles. Even if "money" is not part of your specific result, it could very well be part of the impact. Quantify it.

Let's consider an example.

John is doing data entry as an executive assistant for the CEO of a Fortune 500 company. He writes up reports, does online research, and books meetings for the CEO. In an interview with a potential employer, John gives his STAR story and describes how he created a more efficient schedule and task management system for the CEO. But he doesn't stop there.

With the new task management and scheduling system I developed for the CEO, I was able to save him a significant amount of time and added an extra 4 hours per week to his calendar. While this number may not seem large at first, this has freed up his time to be more involved in hands-on strategy across different departments. Within three months of introducing the new system, the CEO was able to focus his effort on a new product launch that was behind schedule, which ultimately launched on time and became one of our top selling products for the year.

John was able to free up time for the CEO, whose time is valuable. We know that his time is valuable, but John makes a point to explicitly state *how* valuable it was. There was a big product launch and the free time allowed for him to work on this, which he did, and then launched it on time. The company is selling products and making money. John's hard work has helped the company make money by saving the CEO time. We can stop there, and it's a powerful *result* statement for John's STAR story.

Now, be careful not to take a huge leap without substantiation. It would be a stretch for John to say *"I'd like to think that my scheduling system resulted in millions of dollars' worth of revenue for the company."* Correlation does not equal causation. And this sounds a bit like an inflated ego, and while it's good to take ownership for your work, unless you have hard proof then it's best not to take it *that* far. Maybe the CEO would have found time to do it anyways...he probably would have.

<u>The greater point is that John can attach meaning to what he did. Why it was important and the impact it had.</u> He didn't just "make a system and save time," he took his story one step further to articulate what the CEO was doing with that time, which was ultimately beneficial for the company.

The impact of failure

People try too hard to impress interviewers. The truth is that if you are always trying to play yourself up, there will be times when you will inevitably exaggerate the truth, which will lead to problems down the line. Problems like a mismatched job description. Or getting in above your head. Or a company thinking you have a big ego and unable to deal with failure and tough times.

Negative feedback stings. Losing your temper sucks. Not double-checking your work and upsetting a customer is not fun. But they are all learning experiences. When talking about your failures, don't half-ass it or make them seem less impactful than they were. Just like talking about success, we need to thoroughly describe the effects of our failures.

This might seem counterintuitive at first. But if you are describing your failure, then the only way to convey that you took ownership for it is to describe what the results were.

Your ego will try hard to spin this around. Your biggest weakness will become "I'm too much of a perfectionist." Your big failure which resulted in 40% of the company getting pissed off at you is somehow spun to be a positive thing. It was a learning experience, at best, but it was not a *good* thing. Things don't always have to be good...they are never always good. This is not Disneyland.

If making money is the impact of success, then losing money is the impact of failure. Failure can take on various forms that may even seem more opaque when trying to connect them to money. Some are obvious. Let's take some examples:

-You hired the wrong person, and they left in 9 months. How much did it cost to hire them? Did it affect company morale? Did that negative impact result in fewer sales or other people leaving?

-You upset a customer. Did that result in a lost sale? Negative word of mouth that resulted in decreased market share and people switching over to competitors?

-You didn't speak up when you saw a problem. Did this

result in a suboptimal product being released that shouldn't have? Did it result in a problem not being addressed? If it was addressed would you have saved/made money for the company? How did it affect other people around you?

-You didn't test your assumptions. Did this result in decreased sales? Did it take longer to do something because you wasted time making an assumption that you could have checked?

Whatever the problem was, it somehow links back to either people or money. In the first situation, you can ask yourself how the affected person impacted the company's ability to make or save money. For example, if you lost your temper in front of your boss, how did that impact the business? This may seem like a moot point or irrelevant to mention. Break it down to a smaller scale and keep it simple. *The emotional outburst between my boss and I caused unnecessary tension with was a distraction that ultimately took away from my productivity and time, which I could have used to work on X project.*

Rock-STAR Status

Let's say that you are an employer and meet two candidates. Both have great personalities and are qualified for that job. In terms of sales results, they are practically identical. They have both achieved 20 million USD in sales.

On the surface, it's going to be very hard for the interviewer to decide which person is more qualified and who they should hire. The main differentiation is going to come from how the candidates describe their experience. Whoever can provide a more convincing, detailed, and powerful story is going to get the prize.

Upon further discussion, Candidate A describes that he achieved USD 20 million in sales with a team of 5 people who did a lot of the work, and the "achievement" was him checking reports and managing operations. Candidate B achieved the target with a team of 2, acquired five new clients and brought in 50% of the revenue on his own, and has several STAR stories about his own deals that he closed. Candidate B is the candidate of choice despite the "results" being the same as Candidate A's.

<u>The good news is that the STAR Method levels out the playing field.</u>

Perhaps you are not the most expressive person or come from a company nobody has ever heard of. So what? With the STAR Method, you have a chance to describe your story and results in a way that is relatable to the interviewer. Where an interviewer may not have considered you a strong candidate from the start, the STAR Method allows you to reveal yourself as a "diamond in the rough." STAR favors the great.

On the other hand, the STAR Method will not favor people who are trying to fake their way through a story. Even if you are a great storyteller, interviewers are going to ask you "why" and dig into the details. It will become apparent very quickly whether or not your story adds up. In the end, they will likely conduct reference checks and the truth will be revealed.

To achieve rockSTAR status, you don't have to look like a rockstar or work at a rockstar company. You just have to be able to accurately describe your story with as much detail as possible.

STAR Example

*How do you define yourself amidst criticism (asked by Jack and Susy Welch)? *Alternate Question text: How do you stay true to your identity amidst criticism?*

Situation

Situation

My first job after business school was to lead a product development team at Acme Corporation. One of my responsibilities involved weekly product planning meetings that chose product features. After the meeting, I would meet with my staff and delegate programming tasks. Since I am an experienced programmer, I would explain the approach to each feature to be programmed. I expected my staff to write the programs in C++, then test and debug them. We seemed to work very well as a team.

Task

Three months later, my manager collected feedback from my staff. In my performance review, my manager noted that I could improve my delegation skills. His comment surprised me. I thought I was good at delegating, as I would explain my expectations and all necessary steps to each staff member. I felt my staff was productive and consistently benefitted from my coaching. I thanked my manager for the feedback and promised to reflect on my delegating style and consider a change."

Action

Upon reflection, I noticed two issues with my delegation approach. Firstly, in assigning tasks to my staff, I only described the steps they needed to take. I had habitually failed to describe the background of product features we wanted to develop and explain how their work would contribute to and improve the overall product. My staff would just do what I had asked of them without understanding the context of their efforts. Secondly, while explaining how to complete each assignment, I was micromanaging. This may have limited my staff's initiative and reduced opportunities to advance their programming skills. During the next staff meeting, I thanked them for the feedback and acknowledged I would change. From that point forward, each week I explained each product features unique context, described the task in terms of outcomes, and asked my staff how we could approach each task.

Result

My staff was very excited by the opportunity to propose ideas, brainstorm, and choose their own preferred method of going about their work. They were no longer working on my idea alone: they shared in its conception and approached it their way. They were more enthusiastic about their work and realized they were an integral part of something bigger than themselves. During the next quarterly meeting, my manager praised me for empowering my team.

CHAPTER 6:

PIECING IT ALL TOGETHER

"I will not lose for even in defeat/There's a valuable lesson learned so it evens it up for me."
-Jay Z, Blueprint

What is the purpose of the question?

What is a *"wrong"* example? Maybe something that happened ten years ago with a skill that you no longer have, about how you were involved in the development of the precursor to the internet, ARPANET, is not be as relevant nowadays as it was, despite the fact that it was a fantastic achievement at the time.

Listen carefully to what the interviewers are asking. Why are they asking you this question?

If they are asking you about "a time when you dealt with high-pressure situation", then you can assume that the job is likely to have some high-pressure situations. If they are asking you about how to deal with unhappy customers, you can predict that this issue has probably affected the specific job you are applying for.

Take note of all of this because it's indicative of the type of job that you are getting yourself into.

Where could this go wrong? If your STAR story doesn't answer the question and completely misses the point, then you'll either have to find a different example or the interviewer will be frustrated because you didn't understand the question (even though they probably won't say anything to indicate their dissatisfaction).

We want to avoid this, of course. The safest way is to clarify what they are looking for beforehand before diving into your story full throttle.

"So you're looking for an example where I did X?"

<u>Misunderstanding happens often not because you don't understand the question, but because the interviewer is looking for something in particular but phrased the question poorly.</u>

Remember, most interviewers don't have much experience interviewing, so it's your job to help guide the conversation and make sure there are no communication blunders.

Taking it One Step Further - Self Reflection

So you've got a great story. But what did you learn from your experience? Would you do it again? How would you do it differently? Do you just take actions and then forget about them?

These questions are bound to come up. If you are simply telling a good story and describing it, even if it's thorough and logical, it does not mean that you've learned anything.

The best answers and stories teach us something. What

did it teach you? What did you learn from the experience? Reflection is a sign of wisdom.

"Looking back at it, I could have done X and X differently. It taught me ..."

For every example that you've created now go back and think about what you would have done differently and what you have learned.

Throughout the process of outlining and brain dumping, you probably started to reflect already. You had to ask yourself questions like, "Why did I take this action?" or "Why did I choose x and not z?" Those questions most probably led you to certain realizations about how you work and how others work.

Hopefully, you realized some of those things during the time they happened, but often it takes time to digest the experience and to learn from it truly. Sometimes it takes a different way of framing to change our behaviors. Changing behaviors is difficult stuff, especially when they are our own.

Digging for Details

You might need to do some serious digging to nail not only the situation but your full story. How can you trigger your memory to remember certain details of a story that might prove important?

Some tips that might help:

- Look back at old notes, papers and emails. The simple act of reading through these will often trigger other ideas and spark your memory. If you use Gmail for example, the search function makes it quite easy to find emails based on keywords even if you don't remember all of the details.

- Ask colleagues/friends that were involved during the time. Our memories can often be unreliable. In fact, we usually make up stories based on our feelings, blocking out the negative and playing up the positive. In order to correct for this bias ask someone who was there at the time. *What was your take on the situation? What happened?* Get them to tell the story in their own words.

- Start writing. The act of putting pen to paper has a way of conjuring old thoughts. Once we start writing our dreams from the previous night's sleep, for example, we are more much more likely to remember tonight's dreams.

- Sleep on it. Assuming you are not in a huge rush to pull together a great example/story, give it at least one or two nights. Let your mind rest, and you might find yourself having those sparks of memory the next day in the shower.

- Physical activity. It may seem counterintuitive, but exercise helps improve cognitive function, clears your mind, and helps improve memory. I run almost daily and find it one of the most mentally stimulating times of the day — ideas pop up in machine-gun rapid fire as I pound on the treadmill. Or yoga and meditation. Make sure to have your phone or notebook nearby to jot down notes.

- Visit the scene. If this is physically possible, visiting

the location where your STAR story took place will quickly trigger memories. The sight, smell, and act of just walking or going to the place is intertwined neurologically with that story.

The Worst Answer is No Answer

Interviewer: John, can you tell me about your biggest achievement to date?

John: Hmmm...All of my projects have been cancelled and we are always scrambling to get resources for the company. Honestly I can't think of anything I'm really proud of right now. I guess I haven't really made any big strides yet...

That's clearly a terrible way to answer a question. If you don't have your biggest accomplishment prepared, then you might as well cancel the interview and stay home. There's no sensing wasting your time and other people's time.

But sometimes you will get a question that stumps you. Or a question where you need to think about transferable skills or stories that might be relevant to what the interviewer is asking. This may not pop up into your head immediately, which is fine.

There is no rule that you have to start spit-firing a STAR story.

It's perfectly OK to take a minute to think. You can say, 'Sure, give me a second to think of an example.' The interviewer isn't going to think less of you. They will respect you for taking time to think before you speak.

Not answering the question at all is in almost all cases a bad idea. Saying "pass" on the question is a sure way to get yourself disqualified. Imagine if you were working at the company and your boss asked you a question, and you responded with, "Nah, I think I'll pass." It pretty much comes off the same way.

The point is you should always make an effort to answer the question. Now if the question doesn't apply to you, you should make that clear. If you're being asked X but you weren't doing X, explain that but offer up something else you could talk about.

But what if you really just can't think of an example? Fortunately, you can come up with over 50 examples from a handful of stories. Here's how.

How to Answer 55 Different Questions with only 5 Stories

Unless you have weeks to prepare and a photographic memory, it's going to be difficult to write out the details of 5 different stories and expect yourself to recall them during an interview. Fortunately, that's not necessary.

When answering a behavioral interview question and sharing your story, many people make the mistake of saying what they "would do" or "could do." This leaves a lot of room for imagination but falls short of showing what you've actually done. It's easy to fall into this trap if you don't have a specific example that comes to mind. You might panic and think "that's never happened to me, I don't have an example." Making something up is worse than not answering a question.

It should be clear by now, the simple technique is to answer with specific details and a specific story. Now, there is no way that you can prepare for all of the possible questions or behavioral questions that an interview is going to ask. But we can get a little bit creative.

You don't need to reinvent the wheel.

Let's break apart the following example and see what "other" questions this could potentially answer. You've spent a lot of time and effort to dig up details to recount a story. You can use the same example to answer different questions from different angles.

Let's say you are describing your biggest achievement – hitting a 1 million dollar sales target. It's likely that a LOT happened over that three month period for you to get there.

What other stories can we pull from that achievement? Ask yourself the following questions:

- Did I show leadership?
- Did I use data?
- Did I have a strategy?
- Did I delegate?
- Did I improve a process?
- Did I take constructive feedback?
- Did I meet a tight deadline?
- Did I face any tough transitions?
- Did I get outside of my job description to get things done?
- Did I demonstrate exceptional customer service?

- Did I think outside of the box?
- Did I convince any internal stakeholders to make a change?
- Did I change my communication style?
- Did I try a new, innovative idea?
- Did I set a goal and action plan?
- Did I turn a problem into an opportunity?
- Was my integrity challenged?
- Did I disagree with the way things were being done, and took a road less traveled?
- Did I make an unpopular decision that led to success?
- Did people disagree with me?
- Was I tenacious?

Dig deep into your biggest achievement and see if you can pull any other stories out. I am confident that there are at least 5-10, if not more, stories that you can create.

<u>When I say "stories", you will ultimately be using the same story. You are just framing the situation differently and sharing the relevant details for that question.</u>

Now when the interviewer asks you, *"tell me about a time you had to set a strategy"* you can pull from the basics of your STAR story and talk about your biggest achievement, where you also set a three month strategy. And where you showed integrity, thought outside of the box, and had to deal with upset customers. One story has dozens of other lessons packed inside.

Pick four more stories that are strong and detailed, and you can come up with another ten competencies, lessons, and other stories that you can create. There are your 55+ stories.

The question that you may ask is, which five stories should I choose as a base? Typically behavioral interviews fall into a few categories. I suggest you pick a story that represents one of the "Big 5" and then trickle down another few dozen stories from there.

- **Biggest Success/Achievement**
- **Hard Skills** (Sales, Marketing, Organizational Skills, Management Skills, Engineering Expertise)
- **Interpersonal Skills** (Teamwork, Dealing with Tough Customers, Communication Ability, Taking/Giving Feedback)
- **Work Ethic** (Showing Tenacity/Resilience, Humility, Integrity, Patience, Initiative, Honesty, Handling Stress, Handling Change, Working on Tight Deadlines/High Pressure)
- **Growth** (Dealing with Tough Times, Taking Negative Feedback, Learning, Inventing, Showing Creativity, Eager to Improve)

You can download a brainstorming template to get started at **https://starinterviewmethod.com/resources**

Stay Positive, Stay Humble

Often people will belittle their own achievements. It's funny if you are a stand-up comedian. Less so if you are trying to get a job.

You might say, "I haven't achieved anything that great" or "it wasn't a big deal." Don't be so modest. In reality, your achievement was important for your career, your company, and most likely both. The point of good, clear storytelling is to show **how** you made an impact and why it was important, along with how it is relevant to the job at hand. In the grand scheme of things perhaps it was just a drop in the pond. It's all a matter of how you frame it.

Tooting your own horn is at the opposite end of the spectrum. Talking about how great your achievement was without acknowledging how people around you were helpful, or not taking full ownership for a failure that could have been avoided through your actions is ultimately going to hurt you.

You can make an interviewer laugh, but it's not the goal here. Demonstrate your abilities and stay realistic. If they laugh, then kudos.

Why, Why, Why

If you don't know your story, I mean if you don't *really* know it, then people will find out. If you fudge the details, or if there is an inconsistency, it will come out at some point.

People have a natural emotional response to good storytelling, but that doesn't mean people are naturally good storytellers. The amount of preparation you are going to need to deliver your story might be 30 minutes or so, but the amount of preparation you will need to nail all of the interviews might be double that.

You see a murder reported on TV. The first question you ask is, *Why? Why did they do it?* We want to know the motive.

125

We will always have more details than we need to share. We simply don't have enough time to share all of them, nor would we want to. It would be redundant and unnecessary.

In the context of an interview, it's critical to have **more details** than you actually make evident. That's the whole point. Most people don't take the time to spend hours writing their STAR stories. But that's how long it will take. It will take hours just to nail down one good story, including the time you need to go dig up extra details and then refining it to a concise story. There is no shortcut.

The story is created partially to answer the questions and partially for emotional appeal. It's very likely that the interviewer is going to ask you follow up questions. It's not just about motives. It's about logic. It's about numbers. It's about your deductive reasoning in particular situations.

The follow-up questions are going to pry into the details of what you said. They might ask, "why did you choose X and not Y?" You want to try to fill in as many gaps as possible, so they don't have to ask those questions. But they still probably will have some questions or follow up.

That is exactly why having all of the details is important — because of what interviewers *could* ask.

After you've written out your STAR stories, go back through each one, and on each step ask yourself the question, why?

Situation - Why did this happen at this point? Why was it a problem? Why was it really an issue? Why did the problem occur specifically and what factors were involved?

Task - Why was I involved? Why was I assigned to that particular role?

Action - Why did I decide to take these actions? What assumptions did I make?

Result - Why was this result important? Why did X happen and not Y? Why did I care? Why did others care? What were the facts? What did I learn? Why was it a failure or success?

Let it Flow

The STAR Method has been around for a while. People know it exists. Many companies use it, which is why you're reading this book. But because many companies know about it they may be expecting you to use STAR Method to answer behavioral interview questions. So don't make it too obvious by saying "the situation was" and "my task at the time was." There is no need to overuse the words "situation", "task", "action", "result", when answering the question.

Your response should flow freely like a *story*. There should be pieces you don't include and pieces that you include depending on the question and the person you are meeting.

The best way is to practice.

"I know you call it 'storytelling,' but I'm still scared of interviewing!"

That's ok. Some fear and anxiety are always going to be there. After all, this is pretty important for you, isn't it? If you don't care at all, then you wouldn't be nervous. Being nervous just means you care enough about the interview to prepare properly!

But caring too much is not a good thing. You can be a great Olympic-level athlete, get to the Olympics, and then choke. Not because you are not physically capable, but because you got nervous and over-thought the competition.

You attached your self-worth to the medal.

The worst thing you can do is to tell yourself "my life depends on this." It most certainly doesn't.

Even though this interview might seem like the most important thing in the world, it's almost impossible to plan out your career. Why? Because the world is changing very, very quickly and what you're doing five years down the line is hard to predict.

And ironically, the more we attach our self-worth to outcomes that we cannot ultimately control, the more we feel out of control.

The point is, life is chaotic. So don't sweat it and stop trying to control what you can't.

With that said, here are some further few realizations that helped me get over my personal anxiety of interviewing.

- **Try again later.** Fortunately, many companies will let you try to interview again later in the future. Especially a larger company like Amazon or Oracle. They have so many departments, HR people and hiring managers that the likelihood of meeting the same one is quite slim if you are applying for a different position. So take it as a learning experience and good practice. Take notes of your interview so you can improve in the future.

- **Jobs aren't that special.** This job may feel like the coolest in the world. Like the dream job. The golden ticket to freedom, or whatever. The harsh reality is that usually it isn't. There are millions of companies doing millions of interesting things, and more than likely there are a lot of jobs n your field that you might not even know about. Most opportunities are not unique, and there will be similar jobs that come up in the future. So don't sweat it.

- **Fake it until you make it.** How can you be great at interviews if you haven't really interviewed before? Of course, you can practice, but ultimately you have to accept that there are countless people who have been in the same situation as you. Nobody knows what you are thinking, and nobody can gauge your full abilities in one meeting. It's simply not humanly possible for them to do that and it's not possible for you to show them within one hour. What is possible, though, is to give them a good impression. The way to do this is through eye contact, a smile, and at least pretending to be confident. It doesn't matter if you are dying on the inside, the feeling will pass. You will survive.

- **Prepare.** Yes everyone says this — that's because it's true. If you have written out five very, very detailed examples and have gone through 55 potential questions that they could ask you using the five questions as outlined above, some good things will happen. You will gain confidence. You'll be less nervous. When someone tries to throw a curveball at you or ask you "why, why, why?" then you have all of the ammunition you need.

- **Watch others.** Spend time watching good storytelling, reading good fiction, and watching YouTube videos of speakers in your industry. Observe your own emotions and feelings. At what point do you get excited? What made them so good? Did you get happy, sad, mad, scared, excited, or have "aha" moments? Did you like it because of its simplicity and elegance? Listening to Winston Churchill or Malcolm Gladwell speak should get you sufficiently pumped up. But it doesn't have to be anyone famous. For example, you could find a person from your field of interest (whether they are higher up or not doesn't matter) that has any recording speaking engagement online (news, documentary, industry event, etc.). Listen to how they describe things and take inspiration.

- **Practice under stress.** Here's the concept: if you practice verbalizing your examples and telling a story in front of the mirror in an air-conditioned room in your PJ's, this is not going to be realistic. The real interview room is going to be different, and you are going to encounter some stressful situations.

Sometimes, interviews don't go quite as well as we hoped. One small thing can throw us off. Perhaps our bus is late. Your kid throws up all over your resume. Or we forgot to iron our shirt. Or there is traffic. Or maybe the room is hot and sticky and you are visibly sweating. Or your stomach really hurts.

Instead of preparing in a vacuum, create some artificial environment for yourself. Practice your STAR stories at 11 pm when you are tired. Or practice them at 5 am before you drink your coffee. Practice them sitting in the sauna. Practice them on the way to work while you're walking and your heart rate is elevated — which it likely will be in the actual interview. Go practice in the zoo next to screeching monkeys.

Alternatively, you can try and recreate what the interview room would be like. Wear a suit or the clothes you plan to wear on the day of the interview. If you have access to an office space with boring white walls, then go practice there. You get the point. Prepare yourself so that when the interview day comes, nothing can stop you.

Oh, and of course share a good story!

Recording Yourself

Johnny Depp never wants to go back and watch his movies for fear of being disappointed. It's not just him, but many artists and actors.

They either have big egos or are just too sensitive.

If you attach too much importance to what you are doing and it gets tied to your self-worth, then you're going to get shattered when things don't work out. My point — you don't want to be like Johnny Depp, trust me. Don't take yourself so seriously.

I hate recording myself, but it works. Any great athlete or speaker records themselves to find out where the "gap" is in their performance, technique, or presentation. If you don't have the time or don't want to practice in front of a friend, then recording yourself is an especially great option.

The first time you listen to the sound of your voice you will cringe. You might be tempted to scamper away and hide under the couch like a sad puppy. Don't worry, after you do this a couple of times you will get used to it. And once you watch yourself and listen to yourself, just remember that not even Johnny Depp could do it. You're a STAR.

Video and audio combined are best, because we are multidimensional beings. A big component of communication is nonverbal.

Writing vs. Speaking

We've been mainly talking about spoken stories and how you can best express yourself. You can easily apply the techniques in this book to written essays. You need a beginning, a middle, and an end. You need to describe things in STAR.

The great advantage you have here is that you can sit and ponder the question much, much longer and there is no pressure to answer in a given amount of time. If you have taken the time to write out your examples, then most of the work is already done for you. You've already written what you're going to say.

Check out a free template here at https://starinterviewmethod.com/resources/ for getting started with your written STAR story.

How to Answer a Question with STAR

Piecing it all together, here are the steps to answering a STAR question.

- Listen to the question. Why is the interviewer asking this? What are they really looking for?
- Clarify the question and what kind of example they are looking for, if necessary.
- Pick your most relevant STAR story.
- If the interviewer interrupts to clarify a point, take it as a hint and make sure to include that level of detail moving forward.
- Keep your story under 2-3 minutes. Pace yourself.
- After you finish, ask "Did that answer your question?" Ask the interviewer if they have any questions and clarify if they missed any points.

CONCLUSION

The way that we look for jobs — the entire job search process — is changing rapidly. It's largely due to the fact that everything has shifted to the online world. Additionally, the nature of jobs has changed drastically. We've moved from being in cubicles to working in shared offices, collaborating with teams remotely, and taking on more than one job in the gig economy.

Despite these technological advances, finding and interviewing for jobs remains opaque and inefficient. It's become even more confusing and difficult to stand out from the crowd. Why? There are simply too many variables and biases at play to make it a truly efficient way to hire people. Nobody has been able to figure it out — interviewers and interviewees alike.

There are 7 billion individuals on this planet and counting. Many of them will be getting access to the internet in the next few years, and we're going to have a lot of new ideas, companies, and people looking for jobs.

We don't know what is going to happen next.

Fortunately, the same technologies that brought us here can realistically make interviewing a lot less subjective and more reliable. With the advent of blockchain, virtual reality, and progress in neuroscience, in the future you might not even have to go to an interview. Your qualifications for the job will be assessed by a decentralized system with ratings from everyone you have worked with in the past, you will participate in cyber-simulations of on-the-job scenarios, and your mental ability and motivation for the job will be assessed via a neural-linked brain scan.

This might become in our future -- Elon Musk is working on it. I'm hopeful.

But for now, we need to continue telling stories. We need to describe what we have done in as much detail as possible so that we are understood. Some stories are more interesting than others, but for us, the purpose is the same. We tell them so that the listener understands what we are saying and can better understand what it is like to be in our shoes.

The STAR Method is just one way to answer questions — albeit a damn good way, but it's not going to solve all your problems. Storytelling is the best thing we have. After all, we're human.

I hope that this book can take you one step closer to achieving your goals. If you enjoyed the book, I'd sincerely appreciate taking two minutes to write a review on Amazon.

Lastly, I've provided some bonus material and several STAR story examples below. For resources and templates you can check out starinterviewmethod.com/resources.

Feel free to reach out anytime and I would love to hear your stories. My email is mishayoucandoit@gmail.com

Good luck!
Misha

STAR STORIES

1. ORGANIZATION OFFICER

Situation

I was the National President of the American Marketing Association (AMA) for students back in college. The AMA sponsors collegiate chapters for those who are interested in entering the marketing profession upon graduation. The club has career workshops, guest speakers from different marketing professions, philanthropic activities, and fundraising events. Members also participate in the case competitions and attend the national conferences. Some of the major activities that members look forward to every year are the Midyear and Annual Conventions where members from different colleges gather and the best performing local chapters and students are awarded. During our Midyear convention last year, we booked the hotel venue expecting 300 attendees, but unfortunately, only 185 delegates came. Consequently, our budget for the year has been affected as we had to pay for the extra operational costs.

Task

My main responsibility was to lead the organization and oversee the activities of the executive committee to make sure we delivered necessary programs needed by the members. Given the circumstances, I had to have a back-up plan to make sure that everything that we planned for the year would still push through. We had to re-analyze our cost for every activity and conduct early planning for the Annual convention to make sure we could afford another big event at the end of our term.

Action

We conducted a few meetings to resolve the underlying issue. As the organization's president, I had to make sure that the scheduled activities could still proceed despite the lack of funds. I established some fundraising campaigns such as Fun Run and Recycling Project. We went to various non-member schools and encouraged them to sign up with the club. We also prepared earlier for the Annual convention and sourced cheaper venues and suppliers. We offered early payment promotional campaigns for members to help forecast the number of expected participants.

Result

At the end of the year, all planned activities were conducted. We also recruited five new colleges to join the National Organization and gained additional 600 members. During our Annual Convention, which is the last gathering of members for the year, 420 members attended. This was more than twice the number of our Midyear participants. We were also able to recover our losses and collect enough funds for the rest of our activities and even pay forward funds to the next batch of officers. Personally, it was my biggest achievement so far. It tested and enhanced my leadership skills. I learned to strategize and be quick in thinking of contingency plans, be open to ideas of my co-officers, and work well with a team.

2. CIVIL ENGINEER

Situation

I was in grade school when my family migrated from Vietnam to North Hollywood, California. I lived with my two brothers and my mother who was a school teacher. When I reached Senior High, my mother was diagnosed with breast cancer. She had to stop teaching, incurred a lot of debts, and used all our savings to finance her medication.

Task

As the eldest son, I was responsible for taking care of my younger siblings and my ailing mother. After graduating from high school, I decided to quit school and work to help finance the needs of my family. It was a tough decision as I was always an honor student and everyone thought I had the potential to be an engineer. It was a struggle seeing my classmates do group studies in the coffee shop where I served as a waiter. But it was harder to see my family go hungry and not find a cure for my dying mother.

Action

I worked as a bus driver, waiter, newspaper vendor, and call center agent. I worked from early in the morning until late at night. My younger brothers also offered to help out so every morning I prepare sandwiches for my brothers to sell. We did everything so we could to sustain our basic needs and finance our mother's treatment.

When my mother died after fighting cancer for five years, I decided to go back to school and pursue my dream of becoming an engineer. At that time, my brothers were both working. I became a working student and qualified to be a University scholar.

Result

After 12 years of work, I was able to finally finish college and become a full-fledged Civil Engineer. I was able to pay off all our debts and provide for my family's needs. All my hard work had finally paid off. It was such a rewarding feeling fulfilling a lifelong dream and knowing that I made my mother proud in heaven.

3. MATH ANXIETY

Situation

I was always very active in school activities back in college. I was a Political Science student who enjoyed debates/discussions, reading news, and participating in extracurricular activities. I was also consistently on the dean's list. But the one thing that I could not stand was Mathematics.

Try as I may, I could not avoid Algebra classes. I took all my minor subjects in my first two years but forgot that I still had to take on Advanced Algebra. So in my senior year, I have no choice but to take the course. Unfortunately, I had the most terrifying Algebra professor in school. As I expected, I failed my Midterm exams.

Task

I was concerned that I would not graduate on time because of a minor class. I could not stand getting low grades on my transcript. I studied hard to make sure that I would maintain a good average when I graduate. It would be a shame if I failed a class - I had this anxiety for years.

Action

At this point, I had two options. Option # 1 was to drop the class and delay my graduation. Option # 2 was to make more effort studying, pass the subject, and graduate on time. Each option had its own risks. However, I had no a choice but to pass the class, so I decided to pursue option # 2.

I asked my classmates who were Math majors to tutor me. After class, I stayed in the library for hours and practiced solving algebraic problems. I was so desperate to pass the subject that I posted formulas on the wall in my room to become more familiar with them.

Result

During our final, my goal was just to pass. And when the results were released, I was surprised to find out I got an A in the exam. It was surreal! That experience taught me three things: One, there is always time to overcome a life-long anxiety. Age doesn't matter. Two, with a lot of perseverance and hard work, I can make things possible. Lastly, never be afraid to ask for help. It is impossible to learn everything on your own. Having a support system will make things better and easier.

4. BIKING CLUB

Situation

I have always felt like I was the ugly duckling in my family. Of the three siblings, I have the largest body type. My two sisters participated in beauty pageants while I enjoyed the sitting in the audience eating popcorn. They looked so pretty and sexy wearing cool clothes while I looked like a tomboy wearing my jogging pants and oversized shirts.

People would constantly compare me to my sisters. Some people said that I'm adopted because I have a different body type. I grew up feeling insecure about my weight. When I started college, I began feeling more anxious about my weight. I was 16 years old and I weighed 280 lbs. I fell into a deep depression. I tried many kinds of diets, but nothing worked for me. I was hopeless.

Task

My goal was to lose weight. At that point, I knew I must control my relationship with food and get daily exercise. I felt like this was my last chance to be able to achieve a healthier lifestyle. However, it has not been an easy ride. There are times that I would still crave for sweets and salty chips.

Action

Just when I was about to give up, I joined the Bikers Club. I would wake up at 4 o'clock in the morning and meet my team. We would cruise around the park, our school, and even reached the other neighboring cities. I enjoyed biking, and I forgot about my depression whenever I rode.

Result

What started as a desperate move became a routine. After almost a year of actively participating in biking events, I lost 160 lbs. I felt light, full of energy, and healthy. I gained confidence and improved my self-esteem. It was fulfilling as it did not only helped me overcome my depression, but it made me transform into a more health-conscious individual.

5. CPA BOARD EXAM

Situation

I was a good student back in college. I enjoyed working with numbers and analyzing problems. I was also very competitive, and I represented my school in various accounting and auditing competitions, winning many awards. I graduated with highest honors and got an award for Best Thesis. My professors and classmates expected that I would master the board exam someday.

I was pretty confident that the CPA board exam would be a piece of cake for me. I had won awards and medals when I competed with other schools so a measly exam was no match for me. In my mind, passing the exam was easy, but my goal was to top the list. I felt proud and sure of myself. When the results came, my name was not on the list. I failed. I was shattered.

Task

Those were the darkest days of my life. I could not show my face in public. I felt like I did not only fail myself but my entire college. I locked myself in my room for a month just crying and soul-searching. But life must go on and so did I.

Action

I decided to give it another try. This time, I gave it my best to prepare for my next challenge. It became a motivating factor for me to work double time with my study habits and not to be overconfident.

On the exam day, I prayed very hard. But this time, I prayed with a humble heart. My desire was to pass the exam according to God's will. If things don't go my way, I am sure He has better plans for me.

Result

When the results were released, I was surprised to be the Top 2 among the 10,000 CPA board candidates n our group. Indeed, there are times that we may question God's plans but he will eventually reveal why we went through everything that happened in the past, good or bad.

6. STAGE FRIGHT

Situation

Growing up, I never liked to socialize with other people. I would rather stay home, play my video games and not get distracted by the outside world. While my brothers were playing basketball in our village' clubhouse, I locked myself inside my room reading sci-fi books and magazines. I had stage fright. When I was in grade school, I never participated in school plays or anything that required getting up on stage.

By the time I got to high school, I had become friendlier. I joined the Business Administration Club and became an active member. I also joined the finance committee. When they were looking for the next group of officers, they considered me to run for VP Finance. Being a Math major, I enjoyed numbers, and I thought the position would be a chance to work on my own. However, I quickly remembered that part of running for school office would require me to speak in front of an audience. I started to doubt my candidacy.

Task

Although I had been part of the group for quite some time already and made quite a few friends, my stage fright did not go away. But since I could no longer say no to my group, I had to practice my public speaking skills.

Action

I watched videos on YouTube to learn how to overcome stage fright. I practiced in front of my closest friends. We went to almost all of the BA classrooms, presented our party's platform, and tried to win the votes of the students. We also conducted free mentoring sessions for those who were struggling with their business subjects.

Result

As a result, the majority of the candidates from our party won the election. And the guy who used to be an introvert became the Vice President of Finance. I consider this a milestone in my life as I overcame one of my biggest challenges. I became more confident talking in front of a crowd and even expanded my network. Also, I further developed my interpersonal and math skills as I got acquainted with people who shared the same interests.

7. THE INTERN

Situation

During my last year in college, I worked as an intern in a small law firm. We had a storage room and an office area shared by eight people; 7 full-time employees and one intern. The office has very limited space cluttered with boxes and a bunch of paper documents. There were a few cabinets where we filed confidential cases.

Task

My job required me to do clerical tasks such as photocopying, printing, and typing documents. I also organized papers, labeling each one and filing them inside storage boxes. However, I noticed that sometimes, there are tons of papers that the employees just shred or throw away even though the files don't seem to be confidential. Also, the bulk of boxes in the work area make it hard for employees to move around the office.

Action

I talked to my colleagues about this, and they seemed concerned too. Thus, I talked to my supervisor and suggested we reorganize the paper boxes and sell some of the scrap papers to the junk shop. Thankfully, he was open-minded about the idea. He immediately asked my colleagues to help sort the documents to make sure that only the unimportant files will be destroyed. Since this was my initiative, I looked for scrap paper buyers. I found a company that recycles waste materials into new paper products. We then sold four boxes of used papers.

Result

Consequently, we were able to collect enough funds and used them to buy two second-hand storage cabinets. This project helped reduce waste and de-clutter the office area. The space where the boxes were previously stored was converted into a workstation and is now being shared by two employees. I was very happy with the result of this project as the whole company benefited from it. Personally, I never thought that such an initiative would lead to this huge impact. Indeed, this is proof that small things make a difference. Never underestimate the value of small ideas!

8. WORLD TRAVELLER

Situation

After graduating from college, I wanted to try something new — something I have never done before. I was feeling adventurous, so I decided to plan my first European backpacking trip. I had never traveled far alone. The farthest I had travelled to was when I visited my mother's province located in the Southern part of the Philippines which took roughly 15 hours of traveling by land.

Task

To finance my trip, I worked as a waitress and as a babysitter for six months. I earned a total of $3,500. But of course, I wasn't sure if my savings would be enough for my three months stay in Europe so I thought of ways to stay within my budget. Action

I planned my trip pretty well. I did a lot of research to organize my itinerary. I packed only ten pieces of clothing and just mixed and matched so I could come up with different looks. This was also my way of avoiding extra luggage fees. I allocated a budget for visa and travel insurance. I brought medicines and first aid kits. I stayed in hostels and even tried couchsurfing to control my lodging expenses. I also considered taking different modes of transportation such as buses, trains, and planes, whichever has the least cost. I familiarized myself with public transportation. I downloaded different apps to help me with research and travel. I also rarely dined in restaurants. I ate where the locals eat and most of the time; I bought food in the grocery and cooked them in the hostel to minimize my cost. I brought my own water bottle wherever I went as water in Europe is very expensive. I only went to selected museums and paid attractions. For the most part, I joined free group tours.

Result

After spending three months on the road, I was able to travel to 20 countries in Europe. I met different people from all over the world and experienced different cultures. This experience taught me how to manage my finances better and to work within a very tight budget. Because of my detailed planning, I only spent $3000 which means I saved $500 that I can use on my next trip. I learned a lot on this trip. If you plan ahead, you'll have tons of wonderful experiences but be ready for surprises. Not everything will turn out according to plan, so always be ready with backup plans. Lastly, it transformed me to become an independent and stronger individual. Although traveling alone is very risky, I took the risk and turned a dream into a reality.

9. FREELANCER

Situation

My family lives in the village while I stay in the city to pursue my studies. My only allowance is what my parents send me from selling corn in our hometown. The amount that I receive from them is sometimes not enough to cover my living and educational expenses.

Task

When I was in my junior year in college, my family had a problem with our finances. There was an insect pest that hit our farm. Thus, my parents could not send me money for a time. I tried to look for a part-time job but couldn't find one until I discovered a freelancing site online. I signed up and looked for jobs right away.

Action

Building a portfolio for new freelancers is a challenge. There are thousands of talented freelancers in the market, and it was not easy getting jobs. Luckily, I received my first project as a writer. I was asked to read six academic articles and write a 1 page summary for each of them, within seven days. The contract paid $75. And since I was very excited to book my first job, I made sure to over deliver and aimed at satisfying my client. I finished the project in 3 days and submitted a detailed summary of the articles.

Result

My client was very happy with my work and gave me a $10 bonus. To my surprise, he even gave me another project with a bigger budget. This time, it was enough to cover my current month's expense. I consider this a milestone as it not only helped me with my financial troubles, but it also opened opportunities for my future projects.

10. THE CREATIVE DESIGNER

Situation

During the summer of 2016, I ventured into a business. With the little money I saved from my allowance, I decided to sell ready-to-wear clothes in a bazaar. I found a supplier who is based in Thailand and sells clothes for as low as $1.00. I signed up for a bazaar and sold my goods. However, I over-calculated my purchases and spent $300 for the supplies and set-up of my booth. At the end of the day, I only earned $100 which was not even enough to cover my expenses.

Task

I was very disappointed. Also, I had difficulty storing the clothes at home as I live in a small apartment with my family. I have very little space for my inventory. I tried selling it online but was not able to sell much.

Action

I decided to reinvent the materials. I transformed the shirts into handmade fabric accessories. Since I have a good relationship with my school's administrator, I asked if I could sell them at our school event. I set up a small stall during our Foundation Week and sold all my products. I also crafted personalized designs upon request. It eventually became my source of passive income. I was able to sell in some local bazaars and online websites.

Result

Because of my creativity, I was able to dispose of my inventory by transforming it into a more artistically appealing product. I repackaged it to make it more appealing to students and young professionals. To date, I am earning $500 per month with my side job. I consider this quite an accomplishment because at a young age, I was able to create a business which started out as a part-time. This goes to show that with a good sense of imagination, we can achieve unlimited success.

11. FINANCE PROFESSOR

Situation

I have a BA Fine Arts. I come from a family of artists, so I thought Arts was what I wanted to pursue in my life. However, after graduating, it was a challenge for me to get hired, so I decided to enroll in an MBA program. In graduate school, I met one of the best finance professors who was also the CFO of a multinational bank. I was very impressed with his professional profile and wanted to be like him. I became obsessed with numbers, took the necessary exams, and received my trading licenses.

Task

After finishing my Master's degree, I worked in a few financial institutions. I received a good compensation package and even traded stocks on the side. I was living a good life. I thought I was content with the flow of my career until I started teaching.

Action

I was referred by a colleague to become a part-time professor of finance courses. I had a reputation as a "terror" professor. I gave my students hard problems to solve but did not necessarily fail them. Apart from their textbooks, I provided them online study materials which they could also use at their jobs. I trained them to use advanced Excel, create financial models, and do financial forecasting. I did this because I wanted my students to be prepared to not only pass my class but to succeed with their thesis and future work.

Result

My greatest achievement is being able to see my students succeed in life. Even if I was no longer their professor, they still reach out to me when they need help with more advanced subjects or even in their personal businesses. They thank me for the skills that they have learned and share how they were able to apply these skills for their thesis. Many of them now are managers, supervisors, and even CFOs in their respective companies. I am glad to see my students grow and become successful individuals. Although teaching is not a very lucrative profession, for me it is the most fulfilling.

12. AIRBNB

Situation

Our family lives in a four bedroom apartment located in the city center of Seoul. When my two sisters got married, they left the house and moved with their respective families. As the youngest daughter, I worked as a stylist in an apparel store to help support my parents. But then I ran into some financial difficulty. I was laid-off from work due to downsizing.

Task

Since I was the breadwinner in my family, I thought of other ways to earn money until I got my next job. I had no luck finding a full-time job and I knew I needed to use my skills and our existing resources to make a living.

Action

Then I found out about Airbnb. I did lots of research and decided to offer my sisters' former bedrooms for $25 per night. Using the little money I saved, I re-designed the rooms to make them more pleasant for our guests. I used my skills as a stylist to make the rooms comfortable, stylish and fun. I also paid for WiFi and other essentials. As an added touch, I left welcome baskets in each room.

Result

Because of the transformation I made and the service we rendered for our guess, we received good reviews. For the first two months, we only had three bookings. But because of the good reviews, I managed to accommodate 12 bookings in a month for both rooms. My parents and I felt overjoyed with how this all turned out. We were able to finance our everyday living expenses, and as a bonus, we got to meet new people from very different parts of the world. Most of our clients are referrals from previous customers, and I still keep the business even though I now have a full-time job.

13. PROJECT MANAGEMENT

Situation

Our company is engaged in selling Solar PV Systems to both public and private firms. One of our major projects during the year was to deliver solar PV system to roughly 4,000 remote areas all over the country. The project started in June 2016 and ended in April of the following year.

One of the biggest challenges we encountered was the delay in the delivery of mounting structures and solar batteries. Our main supplier could not finish the fabrication of materials due to a lack of supplies. At that time, I was concerned that I might disappoint the management and that the customers will be dissatisfied with the outcome of our work.

Task

As the project manager, I had to make sure that everything is in place. I monitored the status of the project and generated reports for management. I assigned tasks to our team and made them accountable for their respective project roles. As a group, we had to make sure that our project reports were complete and that we kept open communication within the team.

Action

To resolve the issue, I sourced for other suppliers and asked if they could deliver the materials within the specified due date. I found one who has bigger and better machines to better accommodate our orders. After that, I collaborated with my logistics team to make sure that the materials would be delivered as soon as the suppliers finished production.

Result

As a result, we were able to deliver and install the Solar PV systems two weeks ahead of the deadline. The families located in those 4,000 remote areas now enjoy the benefits of having both light and energy in their homes. This was my biggest project so far in my career in project management. It transformed me to become a fast thinker and become more strategic in implementing a project. It made me realize the value of open communication and teamwork in making things possible. Despite all the issues that we have encountered, we still managed to deliver. The challenge is what made it great.

14. LOGISTICS

Situation

I worked as a management consultant in a company with business interests in personal care and food manufacturing, marketing, and distribution. One of the major problems at the company was in their logistics department. They had nine trucks and 15 truck drivers. The had have no definite schedule of delivery. The current setting was that whoever was available was asked to deliver the products to a specific location.

Task

The company allocated 6,000 Taiwanese dollars (TWD) per delivery trip of their truck drivers inclusive of all travel expenses from warehouse to selected destination. The owners thought that it is a very generous amount, so they asked for my professional help.

Action

The first thing that I did was to audit the breakdown of expenses being provided by the drivers. I found out that the majority of the expenses went to oil and tolls. Given the circumstances, I recommended that the drivers' activities be monitored to develop a more precise delivery schedule. I established a "Cashless Policy" to almost every transaction to better manage the expenses of the company. I asked the owners to partner with oil stations who can accommodate cashless fuel purchases. I also installed prepaid toll passes in every unit. I then installed

GPS trackers to ensure the safety of company assets and inventories. Lastly, I budgeted TWD 100 per meal which is the average price of a meal in Taipei.

Result

At the end of the project, my client's logistics costs dropped to TWD 1,800 per delivery trip. They were very satisfied with my recommendations not only because of their cost savings, but it also improved the existing process. Upon completion of the project, they referred me to more job assignments within and outside their organization. This is why I am passionate about business consulting. Apart from flexible working hours and good pay, I get a rewarding feeling helping entrepreneurs grow and build their businesses.

15. UBER DRIVER

Situation

I was employed as a family driver for nine years for a Chinese family based in Kuala Lumpur. I have two children who are both in high school while my spouse is a stay-at-home mom. I was the breadwinner, so I was responsible for providing the needs of my family. Unfortunately, most of the time, my earnings were not enough to sustain our basic needs.

Task

Every day, I would wake up at 4 o'clock in the morning and get ready to pick up my boss and his kids to take them to work and school. I worked six days per week from Monday to Saturday. Most of the time, I would go home after midnight especially whenever my boss worked overtime. I was earning MYR 1,200 in a month. My employers were very nice to me, and I had no personal issues with them. My only concern was the demanding work schedule and low pay. My kids were going to college soon, and I needed to provide for our daily needs and their educational expenses.

I had friends who were already Uber drivers. They told me how much they were earning just by using the famous mobile app. I thought of trying it but could not afford a brand new car. Fortunately, my nephew offered to sell his six months old car to me with payments on an installment basis for the next three years. I gladly jumped at the offer.

Action

Eventually, I left my job. Driving for Uber, I have a different schedule. I would leave home at 8:00 in the evening and go home at 5:00 in the morning. I avoid the traffic and peak hours. I try to get at least 20 bookings within three days so I can get a MYR 250 bonus. I also make sure to provide good customer service so I can get a 5 star rating for every ride.

Result

Currently, I earn an average of 2,000 – 2,500 MYR per month. I have enough money to finance my children's education and meet my family's economic needs. I can also afford to make monthly car payments from my earnings. I have a flexible working schedule so I get to spend more time with my family. Working for Uber has been an amazing experience, and I will always be thankful for this opportunity.

16. PEOPLE MANAGEMENT

Situation

Our company is an Oil Distribution Company which distributes filtration products for the industrial and marine market. It was established in 2015 and has a total of 15 employees composed of sales, accounting, marketing and engineering experts. It has a flat organizational structure where everyone reports to the owner. None of the employees have a defined job description or performance metrics.

Task

My role is to supervise the team. My main responsibility is to oversee the operations of the business and ensure that we meet the expectations and needs of customers and clients. However, I noticed that for the past six months, most of my staff does not seem to be busy with their tasks. I see them loiter around the workplace and do non-work related tasks. I decided to talk to them and ask for their inputs. They said that part of the problem is that they do not have a specific job description. They do not know the boundaries of their responsibilities and sometimes do things that are not fit for their skills.

Action

I discussed these issues with our HR team to help me resolve the issue. We revised the organizational structure and drafted detailed job descriptions for each team member. We also re-evaluated our employees and placed them in teams where they can better apply their competencies. KPIs and KRAs were also established to help us quantify the performance of the team. Lastly, I deployed *Activity logs* so I can monitor their daily productivity.

Result

As a result, we became a more structured organization. The people can now focus on their specific tasks and not wait until something is assigned to them. I established accountability and gave performance rewards for great performers and performance plans for under-achievers. I was also able to reduce our team from 15 down to 10. Those in redundant positions were transferred to our sister company to further utilize their skills. Overall, it became a better place to work because people know what to do, they feel more empowered with their job titles, and the employees are more aligned in achieving the goals and vision of the firm.

17. SALES: SOLAR COMPANY

Situation

Because of my passion for renewable energy, I worked as a Sales Representative for a Solar Company. I was trained with how solar energy works and its advantages to the community. Solar has a lot of potential for growth in business as well as in the conservation of the environment. The challenge is not many people know how it works and even if they do, they think that it is costly to invest in a Solar PV System. Also, the competition in the market has been very tight and a lot of companies battle for a lower selling price.

Task:

As part of the sales team, my work is to close deals and inform people about the perks of having a solar energy at home and in their businesses. Our Solar PV system is being sold on a "package" scheme meaning apart from the Solar Panels; the security system is also included to make sure it will work and last longer. Because of this, the owner prices our products and services higher than the rest of the competitors. Although we are very confident about the quality of our services, our salespeople struggle to close more deals because of the high price as compared to our direct rivals.

Action:

With these issues in place, I knew I had to strategize to be able to close more deals. I talked to the owner and asked if we can "unbundle" the package and offer the security system for an extra fee for buyers who intend to avail it. Through this, we would be able to lower the price and make it more comparable to the market price and deliver a minimum viable product that customers need. The owner was quite skeptical at first, but I gave him the pros and cons of sticking to the current scheme. He eventually agreed to my idea, and it was implemented.

Result:

I consider this my greatest achievement as not only have I been instrumental to increasing sales for our company but I also helped in spreading awareness of using renewable energy. It became easier for our sales people to offer our products and services and to provide the customers just what they specifically need without sacrificing quality. It was a learning experience for the entire company to offer the minimum viable product and to leverage on our core competencies. Nothing compares to doing what you love and learning and earning from it at the same time.

18. CUSTOMER SERVICE: WEBSITE INQUIRY MANAGEMENT

Situation

I work as a customer service representative for a family-owned ship-building company. It has been operating for over 60 years, and the average tenure of employees is more than 20 years. The culture is family-oriented, and the processes are still very traditional. It is owned by a Chinese family who is very hands-on in overseeing the entire operation of the company. Part of the business's goal is to become an exclusive distributor of European and US branded Marine engines. There are eight categories of our products and services namely: Marine Engines and Generator Sets, Parts, Service, Customer Training, Boats and Vessels, Boat Supplies, Navigation and Communication Equipment and Automation. Each of these is handled by department heads, and they report directly to the owner. They need to ensure that the owners are copied on all the communications being made to suppliers and customers. Also, all website inquiries are being sent directly to the owners and they, in turn, forward it to the rightful department heads and customer service representative.

Task

My responsibility is to handle queries from customers received via phone call, fax, walk-ins, and email. I act as liaison to provide product/services information and resolve any emerging problems that our customers might face with accuracy and efficiency. I also validate queries and forward them to our engineering experts to better give them the right specifications of services they need. One of the issues that I encounter in my job is that some emails that are being forwarded by the owners are already aged, meaning messages were received at least six months ago. Therefore, it might be useless to answer the queries which will lead to loss of potential sales.

Action

As a concerned employee, I analyzed the existing set-up of the company in managing queries. I designed a new website inquiry system and collaborated with our IT expert in integrating the proposed system on our website. I created a platform wherein there is an option for the customer to tick the category type of their inquiry. Once activated, these queries will be sent directly to our department heads while the owners are copied in the email notification. This way, the owners can still keep an eye on the communication trails, and at the same time, queries will be handled directly by the right team. My role as customer service is to monitor whether the queries are answered on-time and to follow up in case they still have not responded in a week.

Result

This project made a huge impact in optimizing our website inquiry system. From a company who is very used to manual processes, this opened an opportunity to pursue more creative ways of doing things using technology. I consider this as my greatest achievement so far in my career as I managed to facilitate a significant change for the company. This project helped in reducing time in handling queries and managing customer queries. Most of all, I was recognized and applauded by the owners as I assisted them in reducing their daily workload.

19. GOVERNMENT: BID MANAGEMENT (FINANCIALS)

Situation

I work as a finance analyst in an aviation company. Our business mostly caters to other businesses (B2B) and government (B2G). A big portion of our income comes from government transactions by participating on government bidding.

Bid Management is very tedious due to a bulk of technical requirements and strict government regulations. We are required to submit the exact specifications in the bid and ensure that we will not over or under deliver. One of the most important portions of the package is the financial documents.

Task

Our engineers are responsible for completion of technical requirements while the finance analyst is responsible for the financials. We work hand in hand to make sure that we will submit what is expected by the client.

Action

As a finance professional who has a strong experience in financial analysis, I was able to create a financial model suitable for government bids. Instead of manually encoding numbers into the excel sheet, I created a more sophisticated financial model that requires very minimal inputs.

Result

As a result, this initiative made the bidding preparation so much easier, faster and more seamless. It avoided financial errors; ensure accuracy of the numbers and increased chances of winning bids. So far, this is my greatest achievement in the company as it greatly helped in the operations as more time can be devoted to the preparation of technical documents rather than spending more time in doing the financials thus reduced overtime cost.

20. IT COMPANY: CUSTOMER RELATIONSHIP MANAGEMENT

Situation

Microbase Corporation is a solutions and services provider focusing on IT Security and Network Management. I work as a Marketing Officer for the company, and I ensure that the sales team is equipped with enough Marketing tools to promote the end-to-end products and services of the company. One of my responsibilities is to develop and maintain the company's Customer Relationship Management (CRM) system. CRM is a tool that lets the user store customer and prospect contact information, identify sales opportunities, record service issues, and manage marketing campaigns, all in one central location making information about every customer interaction available to anyone in the company who might need it.

In our company's current set-up, Team A, also known as the Sales & Marketing Department, are the only ones with access to the CRM system. The reason is that originally, the Sales team only composed of Team A and Marketing. As the company grew, Team B and C were formed, but they were not given access to the system.

Task

Our sales team is divided into three groups; Team A's accounts are composed of Hardware and Software, Unified Communications, Data Center Solutions and

Network Security, Network Infrastructure and Data Center Management. These are all the high-value products being offered by the company. Next is Team B which is also known as the supplies and parts department. This team focuses on selling computer parts and printer supplies such as toners, mouse, etc. Lastly is Team C or the technical department. This team on the other hand sells maintenance and after-sales services. Every time that Teams B & C has queries about customer history, they will need to contact the Marketing team and ask for certain details to be provided that are found in the CRM system. In a day, we receive at least 15 queries from different sales representatives asking for existing customers' accounts. Due to the bulk of emails and workload, our team could not answer their queries promptly. It sometimes becomes a cause of misunderstanding in between teams and loss of potential sales.

Action

As a Marketing officer who oversees the productivity of my team, I recommended opening the CRM system to the other teams, B and C. Our team should be more focused on promoting our products and developing marketing plans. I asked our IT personnel to provide CRM access to all our salespeople. We discussed the pros and cons of the recommendation and eventually agreed to share the CRM to the entire Sales team.

Result

The Sales (Team A, B and C) and Marketing team were very excited about this newly approved proposal. For my marketing team, it significantly reduced the number of emails and queries being received from the sales team. If before, it took 2 hours a day to check their internal and external emails, now, it was reduced to 1.25 hours thus, giving more focus on enhancing marketing campaigns. As for sales team, it lessened the communication trail as it gave them direct access to the CRM system. It helped them identify and add new leads, gained a better understanding of their customers and it made cross-selling and upselling opportunities easier. Also, it gave them a chance to win new business from existing customers. Lastly, it helped improve our products and services by improving our offers, spotting problems early and identifying gaps.

21. YOUTUBE: VLOGGING

Situation

I am a Korean American living in South Korea. I graduated with a BA in Broadcasting from the University of California at Berkeley. Because of my love for film and editing, I pursued creating my own YouTube channel. When I started in YouTube in 2009, I only had 300 followers in my first year. I wasn't getting enough followers or sponsorships. I had friends who are doing it full-time, but since I could not afford to do the same, I just considered it as a part-time job.

Task

I worked as an on-air personality and content creator for Seoul's Traffic Broadcasting System. I loved what I did and I was used to doing it on a daily basis. However, through the years, I have had a change of heart. I am starting to be more passionate about doing video blogs for my YouTube channel as it reflects more of my personality and skills.

Action

In 2011, I decided to leave my work at the radio station and become a full-time YouTuber. Apart from my main channel which talks about my everyday life and K-beauty reviews, I created another channel for my travelogues. I posted videos every day on my main channel and twice a week on my second channel. I also collaborated with my fellow YouTubers and attended more YouTube and client events in almost everywhere around the world. Also, I collaborated with various K-beauty companies where I helped promote their products and provide reliable reviews for my viewers.

Result

Doing YouTube opened more opportunities for me as a content creator. In three years, I was able to increase the number of my subscribers to 800,000 followers from all over the world. My schedule is more flexible now and I get to travel and meet new people every day. I partnered with a lot of well-known companies and got freebies in return. One of the most memorable collaborations I did so far was when my favorite skincare line called *Innisfree* made me their Beauty Ambassador in the K-Beauty Convention held in Los Angeles, California. It was such a rewarding experience. In the future, I see myself doing more of these collaborations. This profession is not just about showing off but is more of a profession that is worth pursuing.

22. EDUCATION/MOTHERHOOD

Situation

I am a single mother with three children, two boys, and one girl. I am divorced from the father of my kids and was forced to raise them on my own as I was not getting any financial support from my ex-husband. I've been busy looking for teaching jobs, and I even asked my mother to take care of my kids while I'm at work.

Task

I am a college professor by profession. My expertise is in Social Sciences. I worked at every school within the University belt. There were times that I would work at three Universities in a day and run for my next class in a different University so I wouldn't be late. I did everything I could to provide for my children. Apart from my work, I also took and finished my Master's degree to be qualified for more teaching opportunities. I was promoted from Level 1 Professor to Department Chairman and eventually a College Dean. Although I was doing pretty well with my career, I felt like I was not giving enough time for my children.

Action

My children grew up in a Christian environment. With the help of my brothers and my mother, I was able to guide my children to the right path and make sure that they grow up as God-fearing individuals. Every time that there was a family event in school, I would ask my mother to go to the event to accommodate them as I couldn't afford to be absent in my class. My children never complained about my absence at their school events. One day, my youngest daughter said to me that her teachers asked if she was an orphan as they have not seen her parents in any of the school events or award programs. I was surprised to hear that. I thought that providing for my children's needs was enough, but I was wrong. It was a life-changing moment that made me realize my shortcomings as a parent. That's when I talked to my children and apologized. After finishing my Master's degree, I took a rest from doing extra-curricular jobs and made sure that I would have enough time to teach my children at home with their homework and allocate some more family time. We would all go on vacation and attend church together.

Result

Despite the hardship of being a single mother, I was able to achieve my dream of becoming a Dean of the College of Arts and Sciences in our University. But to be honest, my greatest achievement is not about my professional life but with my personal life. I have managed to support all of my children as they finished college, pursued their dreams, and became managers of their respective companies. They all have their own families now, and they became responsible parents. During my recent 60th birthday, they surprised me with a party and gathered all my closest friends and relatives. They told me how they value my hard work and that they love me unconditionally. It's a realization that even though I wasn't able to give them a complete family, my love for them will last eternally.

23. OPERATIONS: FOOD CART BUSINESS

Situation

I am a full-time stock trader with three kids and a stay-at-home wife. Stocks can be highly profitable, but most of the time it is a risky venture. This is why my wife and I decided to start our own business. I am not a business professional. I just asked my friends as to which business they think are profitable and they said it is the food business. We decided to set up our own "Sisig" fast food. Sisig is a known Filipino dish made of from pork products, usually seasoned with calamansi (lemon juice) and chili peppers. We invested setting up the stall with all the amenities and necessary equipment and tools for our mini fast food. Our stall is located in a food court area which is near shopping, a train station, and offices. We pay around Php11,000 (USD 220) monthly rent and operate from 8:00 am to 8:00 pm, Monday through Saturday.

Task

As owners, we are responsible for the end-to-end operations, marketing, and financial investment. We hired one employee who can assist us in the operations of the business. For the past two months of operations, we have not been hitting our desired income. When we started, we thought we could earn at least Php3,000-5,000 (USD 60-100) a day. But it turns out that we only earn an average of Php600 ($12) a day which is very far from our anticipated income and cannot not even cover our operational expenses.

Action

With these issues in mind, we decided to hire a business consultant to assist us with the business. She advised us to further analyze our decisions and be open to possibilities. We attended business and skill training to better equip us with the right tools in pursuing the business. We also took our consultant's advice to switch location to further reduce our cost. We decided to set up a small stall at a nearby food park with a rent of only Php3,000 (USD 60) which operates from 4:00 PM to roughly 12:00 AN. The food park is located near a residential area and a couple of high schools. We also offered to sell our products for a very minimal fee or give certain items for free if customers reach a certain amount of purchase.

Result

After operating in the food park for six months, we are slowly recovering our costs and losses. We earn a profit now, and we were able to decrease our operational costs. We also have more time for the family and still monitor the status of my stock investments. For someone who initially did not know about setting up a business, I was able to overcome the challenges with the help and guidance of the right people. As the head of the family, my greatest achievement is that I found a way to provide a more stable life for my family.

ACKNOWLEDGEMENTS

This book would not exist without the feedback, guidance and support of others. I'm indebted to Joseph Lofgren, Iris Crawford, Lauren Albers, Amanda Rudow, Ann Tee, and Casey Wahl for dissecting my book. Each of them gave me advice from different perspectives that proved invaluable. I'm thankful for Donna Tomici's incredible patience in copy editing — my book would not have been readable otherwise. I am grateful to Kris Guzman for her contributions to many of the STAR stories.

I am also grateful for the ideas and feedback from Kyoka Ishioka, Romen Barua, Ahmed Fahim, Jeremy Heights, Chiara Terzuolo, and Christiane Brew. I owe a big thanks to Emi Hashiride, Aki, Pauline Chen, and Daniel Ku for their marketing expertise.

I wouldn't be here without the continued support of my parents, whose positive energy I can feel from hundreds of miles away.

Finally, I would like to thank my amazing girlfriend, Yuka, for always being by my side.

Thanks everyone for making this book possible.

RECOMMENDED READING:

Here is a list of books that have influenced my writing of the STAR Interview. They range from interviewing, psychology, and productivity. Enjoy!

Principles by Ray Dalio

Work Rules by Laszlo Bock

Extreme Ownership by Jocko Willink

How to fail at Everything and Still Win Big by Scott Adams

Power of Habit by Charles Duhigg

The End of Jobs by Taylor Pearson

Blink by Malcolm Gladwell

Never Eat Alone by Keith Ferrazzi

What Color is Your Parachute? By Richard Bolles

Stumbling Upon Happiness by Daniel Gilbert

The 2 Hour Job Search

Grit by Angela Duckworth

The Storytelling Animal by Jonathan Gottschall

Originals: How Non-Conformists Move the World by Adam Grant

Emotional Intelligence by Daniel Goleman

Thinking, Fast and Slow by Daniel Kahneman

CITATIONS

[i] https://www.theatlantic.com/business/archive/2014/08/ the-economics-of-your-face/375450/

[ii] https://faculty.haas.berkeley.edu/odean/papers%20 current%20versions/individual_investor_performance_final.pdf
[iii] http://journal.sjdm.org/12/121130a/jdm121130a.pdf

[iv] Smart, G., & Street, R. (2008). Who: the A method for hiring. New York: Ballantine Books.

[v] http://www.economist.com/node/18557594

[vi] https://www.slideshare.net/PitchDeckCoach/airbnb-first-pitch-deck-editable

[vii] https://greatergood.berkeley.edu/article/item/how_stories_ change_brain

[viii] http://www.pnas.org/content/107/32/14425.full

[ix] http://www.un.org/sustainabledevelopment/blog/2015/05/ most-workers-now-employed-in-part-time-or-temporary-jobs-un-labour-agency/

[x] https://www.upwork.com/press/2016/10/06/freelancing-in-america-2016/

[xi] http://fortune.com/2011/05/05/the-rise-of-the-permanently-temporary-worker/

[xii] https://www.impactinterview.com/2016/12/what-color-is-your-parachute-book-summary/

[xiii] http://drjoedispenza.com/index.php?page_id=Evolve-Your-Brain

[xiv] Word, C. O.; Zanna, M. P.; Cooper, J. (1974). "The nonverbal mediation of self-fulfilling prophecies in interracial interaction". Journal of Experimental Social Psychology. 10: 109–120

[xv] http://www.fishmanmarketing.com/wp-content/uploads/2010/12/Fish-Man-fishman-drawing-fish-head-suit-Illustration-1REV-419x1024.jpg

[xvi] http://www.businessinsider.com/navy-seals-explain-consequences-of-ego-2015-11

[xvii] http://fortune.com/2017/02/13/elong-musk-job-interview-question/

Made in the USA
Coppell, TX
11 May 2024